# Aesthetics

AN INTRODUCTION

# Aesthetics

## AN INTRODUCTION

*George Dickie*

PEGASUS

A DIVISION OF

THE BOBBS-MERRILL COMPANY, INC.,

*PUBLISHERS*

This book is one of a series, Traditions in Philosophy, published by Pegasus in cooperation with Educational Resources Corporation, which has created and developed the series under the direction of Nicholas Capaldi, Professor of Philosophy, Queens College, New York.

The author is grateful for permission to quote from the following:

*The Principles of Art* by R. G. Collingwood, Oxford University Press, New York.

*Art* by Clive Bell, G. P. Putnam's Sons, New York, Chatto and Windus, London.

For Joyce

# Contents

# Preface

THIS BOOK is intended to be an introduction to aesthetics. However, in addition to discussing the problems of aesthetics, I have not hesitated—except in Part V—to put forward my own point of view. In doing so, I hope I have been fair to the theories criticized.

This book differs from most introductory aesthetics books in having an historical introduction. The purpose of Part I is to trace the central, organizing strains of the field and thereby to set the stage for discussion of present-day problems in aesthetics. Part II deals with the concept of the aesthetic, which is the single most important notion in aesthetics today and which has generated considerable controversy. Part III discusses contemporary philosophies, or conceptions, of art. I have had to be selective here and discuss only five theories from among a sizable number of possible candidates. Part IV is even more limited than Part III in its selectivity. In it I discuss four not closely related problems selected from an enormous number of questions in aesthetics. The subject of Part V is the evaluation of art. In order to cover the main accounts of evaluation, I have had to discuss seven theories.

I want to thank those persons who read all or parts of the manuscript of this book. My greatest debt is to Monroe Beardsley of Temple University. He read all the chapters and gave me numerous helpful comments. This book and many of my other projects would not have been possible without his help and encouragement. Both William Hayes of Washington State University and Elmer Duncan of Baylor University read the whole manuscript and each gave me much useful advice. The following persons read and commented helpfully on one or more chapters: Virgil Aldrich of the University of North Carolina, Arthur Danto of Columbia University, Marcia Eaton of the University of Illinois at Chicago Circle, Göran Hermerén of Lund University, Sweden, Hilda Hein of Boston University, Jerome Stolnitz of Lehman College of C.U.N.Y., and Ben Tilghman of Kansas State University. Mrs. Bernadette McBrien and Mr. James Enright read Part I and made many useful suggestions for its improvement. Mr. Timothy O'Donnell and Mr. Daniel Nathan also read the whole manuscript and made a number of very useful suggestions. Special thanks are due to my wife, Joyce, for a great deal of editorial assistance.

GEORGE DICKIE
Evanston, Illinois

# PART I

---

# An Historical Introduction
# to Aesthetics

---

### Chapter 1.  Introductory Remarks

THE PROBLEMS included in aesthetics are many and appear to
be heterogeneous. This makes a study of the literature of
aesthetics a perplexing matter. One of the major aims of
Part I will be to outline the basic historical routes along
which the problems of aesthetics have evolved. Such an outline will serve to orient the reader and to show how various
problems are historically and logically related to one another.
Without such a guide, the problems of aesthetics have the
appearance of being a series of not very closely related
questions.

The questions included within the field of aesthetics have developed out of twin concerns in the history of
thought: the theory of beauty and the theory of art. These
two philosophical concerns were first discussed by Plato.
Although philosophers have disagreed about the theory of
art (roughly, disagreed about how art should be defined),
they have until very recently continued to debate the theory
of art pretty much on the same terms that Plato did. The
theory of beauty, however, underwent a drastic change in the
eighteenth century. Whereas earlier philosophers had discussed only the nature of beauty, eighteenth-century thinkers
began to be interested in additional concepts: the sublime,

the picturesque, and so on. This new activity may be thought of as either breaking up beauty into its parts or supplementing beauty with additional concepts.

At the same time that beauty was undergoing this change, another development was taking place—the concept of the aesthetic was being worked out in the thought of such philosophers as Shaftesbury, Hutcheson, Burke, Alison, and Kant. In general, these philosophers were concerned to develop a theory of taste which would enable them to give an adequate analysis of the *experience* of the beautiful, the sublime, the picturesque, and related phenomena as they occur in nature and art. The notion of *disinterestedness* is at the center of these analyses and is the core of these philosophers' concept of the aesthetic. What seems to have happened is that as beauty was broken up and fragmented, it was replaced by the concept of the aesthetic as one of the two central concerns of philosophers. After the eighteenth century, the word "beautiful" came to be used either as a synonym of "having aesthetic value" or as one of the many aesthetic adjectives on the same level as "sublime" and "picturesque" which are used to describe art and nature. Since the eighteenth century, the twin concerns of aestheticians have been the theory of the aesthetic and the theory of art.

It may seem that the theory of the aesthetic became the prime concern of aestheticians and that the theory of art and the question of aesthetic qualities are simply subsumed under the theory of the aesthetic. The concept of art is certainly related in important ways to the concept of the aesthetic, but the aesthetic cannot completely absorb the concept of art.

The following discussions of beauty, eighteenth-century aesthetic theory, and the philosophy of art are, for the most part, developed by discussing and summarizing the theories of historical figures. This arrangement permits the reader to glean some idea of the theories of, for example, Plato, Aristotle, Shaftesbury, and Kant and, at the same time, to get a sense of how the problems and theories of aesthetics have developed through history. I have been greatly helped in understanding all phases of the history of aesthetics by Monroe Beardsley's *Aesthetics from Classical Greece to the Present.*[1] My discussion of the development of aesthetic theory in eighteenth-century British philosophy relies heavily on a series of incisive studies by Jerome Stolnitz: "On the Significance of Lord Shaftesbury in Modern Aesthetic Theory,"[2] "Beauty: Some Stages in the History of an Idea,"[3] and "On the Origins of 'Aesthetic Disinterestedness.' "[4] On many points I have been helped by W. J. Hipple's *The Beautiful, The Sublime, and the Picturesque in Eighteenth-Century British Aesthetic Theory.*[5]

---

## Chapter 2.  The Theory of Beauty

---

### Plato

CONSIDER FIRST the theory of beauty presented by Plato (428–348 B.C.) in the *Symposium.*[6] The general theme of the *Symposium* is love. Each of the characters in the dialogue gives a speech about love, and the question of beauty arises because it is concluded that beauty is the object of love. Socrates sets forth his view indirectly in his speech by relating a conversation with a woman named Diotima of Mantineia in which Diotima outlines the proper way to learn to love beauty. Instruction should begin at an early age and the young should first be taught to love one beautiful body (a human body) . When this has occurred, it can be noticed that the first body shares beauty with other beautiful bodies. This provides a basis for loving all beautiful bodies, not just one. The learner ought then to come to realize that the beauty of souls is superior to the beauty of bodies. Once the physical

has been transcended, the second spiritual stage is to learn
to love beautiful practices and customs and to recognize
that these activities share a common beauty. The next step
is to recognize the beauty in the various kinds of knowledge.
The final step is to experience beauty itself not embodied in
anything physical or spiritual.

Notice that this process rises through increasingly abstract
levels until it reaches the ultimate in abstraction—the Form
of Beauty. Plato's treatment of beauty here is an example of
his theory of the Forms: general terms such as "beauty,"
"goodness," "justice," and "triangularity" have as their
meaning the abstract entities Beauty, Goodness, Justice, and
Triangularity. A particular, observed physical object or
action is beautiful (or good or just or triangular) in virtue
of its "participation" in the abstract Form of Beauty (or
Goodness or Justice or Triangularity) . Plato therefore draws
a sharp line between 1) beautiful things which are included
within the class of objects that we see, hear, or touch in "the
world of sense" and 2) beauty itself, which exists apart from
the world of sights and sounds in what Plato calls "the intelligible world." The nontemporal, nonspatial Forms are
the real and eternal objects of knowledge. The Platonic
philosophy does not have much use for or interest in the
world of sense, and considers it from a philosophical point
of view to be a kind of illusion. Plato's philosophy as he
presents it does not provide a very favorable basis for either
a theory of beauty or a theory of art as conceived today. For
him beauty transcends the world of sense experience, which
means that the experience of beauty (not beautiful things)
is unlike what would be described as aesthetic experience
today. A philosophical theory which dismisses sights and
sounds as illusory is not likely to have a sympathetic view
of art.

Plato, however, does take an interest in the beautiful
things of the world of sense, even though this interest is
tinged with ambivalence. For example, he tries to discover
the properties that all beautiful *things* have in common.[7]
There are beautiful things which are simple (pure tones and

single colors, for example) and beautiful things which are complex. The simple things have unity in common and the complex things have measure and proportion of parts in common, which is also a form of unity. But Plato does not mean to identify beauty and unity; that is, he does not think that the word "beauty" and the word "unity" are identical in meaning. Something is beautiful in virtue of its participation in the Form of Beauty, and it is simply a discoverable fact (allegedly) that all beautiful things are unified. Unity is an *always accompanying* characteristic rather than a *defining* characteristic of beauty. In fact, Plato's view seems to be that beauty is a simple, unanalyzable property, which means that the term cannot be defined at all and is logically similar to such "primitive" terms as "red." It is frequently maintained that color terms such as "red" are logically primitive (cannot be defined) and that we can learn the meaning of such terms or how to use them properly only by direct experience—by someone pointing to the color and uttering the appropriate color word. So beauty is considered a simple property which a thing may possess in some degree; if a thing possesses beauty, it also always has *another* property, unity.

Plato's emphasis on measure and proportion set an important precedent for all subsequent philosophers. Some of the philosophers followed him also in adopting some version of his theory of the Forms and thought of beauty as a transcendental entity. Other philosophers simply identified beauty with measure and proportion as we find it in our sensuous experience.

## Plotinus

The next philosopher with a fully developed theory of beauty of whom we have much knowledge is Plotinus (204–269 A.D.). Plotinus' philosophy[8] is a version of Platonism in which the mystical potentiality of Plato's philosophy is developed to the fullest extent. The very nature of mysticism is such that it is impossible to make clear by the use of language what is involved in that view. The truths of mysticism are, it is said, ineffable. The primary focus of this philosophy is the One which is the source of all things. Plotinus' mysticism emphasizes even more strongly than Plato's philosophy the illusoriness of the world of sense. Plotinus accepts Plato's theory of Forms and holds that the world of sense to some limited degree "reflects" and thereby reveals the Forms to contemplation. Plotinus, like Plato, holds that the experience of beauty itself is not a sensuous experience but an intellectual one. Perhaps the most pervasive and important result of the theories of Plato and Plotinus was the establishment of the notion of contemplation as a central idea in the theory of beauty and, consequently, in the theory of aesthetic experience. Almost all aesthetic theories have maintained in one way or another that the experience of beauty or, more generally, aesthetic experience involves contemplation. When philosophers such as Plato and Plotinus spoke of contemplation, they meant a kind of meditation in which a person has as the object of his awareness some nonsensuous entity, for example, the Form of Beauty or the Form of Triangularity. There is, of course, another sense of "contemplation" which is something like steadfast attention to some object, which may, of course, be an object of the world of sense. Most modern theories of aesthetics no doubt vaguely intend the latter sense of contemplation, but I think that some of the aura of the Plotinian sense infects the use of "contemplation" in modern aesthetic theories. It is not so much the nonsensuous-object aspect as the aspect of reverent meditation which haunts modern theories. This spiritualistic holdover is probably at least partially responsible for the solemn and pompous attitude toward art and beauty that some persons display. "Contemplation" is one of those highly abstract words which sometimes masks important distinctions. Some experiences of art and nature are properly contemplative—for example, listening to religious music or looking at a statue of Buddha. But a great many of our experiences of art and nature are not contemplative—they are gay, spirited (not spiritual), titillating, humorous, uproariously funny, and so on. It would seem then that if a word is desired which will correctly characterize all our aesthetic experiences, "contemplation" is not appropriate because it is too narrow. Such narrowness is not surprising when we consider that the notion has its source in the views of unworldly philosophers.

## St. Thomas Aquinas

The philosophy of Plato was influential for many centuries. For example, St. Augustine (354–430 A.D.), who was an important philosopher and theologian, perpetuated the Platonic theory of beauty as well as other Platonic doctrines. Almost nine hundred years after Augustine's time, the influence of Aristotle (384–322 B.C.), a student and contemporary of Plato, replaced Plato's influence on Christian thinkers. Aristotle had rejected the Platonic view that the Forms transcend the world of experience and exist in their own distinct realm. Aristotle's philosophy retains the concept of the Forms but maintains that they are embodied in nature as we experience it and that they have no independent existence. For Aristotle there are not two worlds—as Plato held—but only one, and it is perfectly intelligible. For Aristotle the world as we sensuously experience it is in no basic way illusory, and his philosophy provides a basis for an interest in the phenomena of both nature and art.

Within the sphere of Christian theology, Aristotelian philosophy received its most powerful and influential expression in the works of St. Thomas Aquinas (1225–1274 A.D.). Aquinas's conception of beauty is not an unworldly one; he defines "beauty" as "that which pleases when seen."[9] Beauty is also related to desire in that "the beautiful is that which calms the desire, by being seen or known." Of course, not everything pleases and calms desire in being seen or known, and Aquinas attempts to isolate the properties of the objects which do please. He concludes that the conditions of beauty are three: perfection or unimpairedness, proportion or harmony, and brightness or clarity.

Aquinas's theory has both objective and subjective aspects. The stated conditions of beauty are objective features of the world of experience. But the idea of pleasing as part of the meaning of "beauty" introduces into the theory of beauty a subjective element. Being pleased is a property of a subject (a person) who has an experience, not a property of an object a person experiences. Aquinas's introduction of pleasing is a significant step away from the objective Platonic conception of beauty toward a subjective conception. The subjective conception of beauty later reached a high point in the theories of eighteenth-century philosophers.

Aquinas stresses the cognitive (knowing) aspect of the experience of beauty. This means that in the experiences of beauty the mind grasps a Form which is embodied in the object of the experience. Aquinas seems to suggest that there is no single Form or property of beauty which is common to all beautiful things, but rather that the mind grasps or abstracts the Form which causes an object to be what it is. For example, the mind grasps the Form of Horseness when the object experienced is a horse. Of course, as any object whatsoever embodies a Form, the grasping of a Form is not the only thing involved in the experience of beauty. In addition, there are the three objective conditions of beauty which must be met and there is the subjective factor of being pleased by what is seen or known. The experience of beauty is a cognitive one but there is more to it than that, and the object of such a cognitive experience is neither transcendental nor is it the Form of Beauty.

## Ficino and Alberti

The Renaissance led to new interest on all intellectual fronts, an interest which in many respects drew upon the philosophy of ancient Greece. One important movement was the resurgence of Neoplatonism. Marsilio Ficino (1433–1499 A.D.) was a central figure in the movement.[10] Little if anything new is added to the theory of beauty by Ficino. He emphasizes a theory of contemplation which retains the spirit of Platonism. In contemplation the soul withdraws from the body and from interest in bodily concerns, and the objects of contemplation are the familiar Platonic Forms. Such contemplation, in Ficino's view, is not exclusive to the experience of art but is characteristic of this experience.

In addition to philosophical speculation there was great interest during the Renaissance in more concrete and specific topics such as the theory of painting and the theory of architecture. The work of Leon Battista Alberti (1409–1472 A.D.) is a good example of this more empirically oriented activity.[11] Alberti's theory of beauty is simple and straightforward—he defines beauty in terms of a harmony of parts in which any change would be for the worse. This definition seems to entail that beauty is identical with a certain degree of harmony, rather than harmony being a condition of beauty. Alberti's definition is an objective one, as it refers only to properties (actually a single property) of objects and not to any states of mind of subjects (persons). He does, however, postulate a special sense of beauty in persons by means of which beauty is perceived. The notion of a sense of beauty (under a variety of names) is a concept which gained great currency in eighteenth-century aesthetics.

## The Eighteenth Century: Taste and the Decline of Beauty

The eighteenth century was a critical time in the history of aesthetics. During this period a number of British thinkers worked intensively on "the philosophy of taste" and provided the basis for aesthetics in its modern form. About the middle of the century, the minor German philosopher Alexander Baumgarten (1714–1762) coined the term "aesthetics," which in time became the name of the field.[12] Baumgarten's view, however, had very little influence on the subsequent development of aesthetics.

The philosophical tradition of explaining behavior and mental phenomena by attributing each kind of phenomenon to a distinct faculty of the mind had a strong influence on both the rationalists such as Baumgarten and the empiricist British philosophers. The doctrine of mental faculties had been worked out in great detail during the medieval period. According to this doctrine, there are the vegetative faculty (which explains nutrition and procreation), the locomotive faculty (which explains movement), the rational faculty (which explains mental behavior), and the sensory faculties (which explain perception, imagination, and the like). Baumgarten tries to work aesthetics into a scheme of this type by conceiving of it as the science of sensory cognition. He thinks of art as a low-level means of cognition, that is, of gaining knowledge. In short, Baumgarten conceives of art as falling under the domain of both the sensory faculty and the intellectual faculty as a mode of inferior cognition. By contrast, the main tendency of the British philosophers is to subsume the experience of beauty under the sensory faculty alone, conceiving of it as a phenomenon of taste. For them the perception of beauty is not a matter for the external senses like seeing or hearing. By analogy with the theory of the internal senses (memory, imagination, and so on) developed by medieval philosophers, many of the British philosophers thought they had discovered a new internal sense—the sense of beauty.

Prior to the eighteenth century it was generally assumed by philosophers that "beauty" named an objective property of things, either a transcendental or an empirical property, depending on the theory. These early philosophers concluded that objective judgments of beauty could be made, just as we can make objective judgments about red things. But the analysis of beauty furnished by the eighteenth-century philosophers of taste shifts the focus of aesthetic theory. They want to furnish a basis for objective judgments of beauty, but they try to do so by focusing their attention on the alleged faculty or faculties with which men react to certain features of the objective world. The apparatus of taste is conceived of by some of them to be a special single faculty (*the* sense of beauty), by some to be composed of several special faculties (the sense of beauty, the sense of the sublime, and so on), and by some as simply the ordinary cognitive and affective faculties functioning in an unusual way. When only the ordinary faculties are involved, the mechanism of association usually plays a major role in adapting these faculties to the task of experiencing beauty. In short, these philosophers are interested in human nature and its relationship to the objective world. This movement in aesthetics was not an isolated phenomenon but was part of a larger philosophical movement which began with the interest of seventeenth-century philosophers in human nature and the limits of human knowledge. It was hoped that the faculty of taste would be a basis for objective judgment. In the hands of these thinkers philosophy became *subjectivized,* that is, they turned their attention in on the subject (the human being) and analyzed the states of the subject's mind and his mental faculties.

Another important eighteenth-century development was the bringing into aesthetic theory of notions other than that of beauty—for example, the notions of the sublime and the picturesque. This development gave a richer and more adequate theory, but it also made the theory more complicated and less unified. The traditional theory of beauty is highly unified, if for no other reason than it is about one thing, namely, beauty. The disunity caused in the eighteenth century by the fragmentation of beauty set up a tension which was resolved over a period of years by the development of the concept of the aesthetic. For better or worse, this concept furnished a unified theory and reestablished equilibrium. The establishment of *aesthetic* theory as the theory that unifies the problems of the theory of beauty and the philosophy of taste was not completed in the eighteenth century. However, the views of the German philosopher Kant, published near the end of the eighteenth century, incorporated the insights of the British aestheticians and came close to being a unified aesthetic theory. By "aesthetic theory" I mean a theory which makes the concept of the aesthetic basic and defines other concepts of the theory in terms of the aesthetic.

In addition to the appearance of competing concepts, another reason for the decline of the theory of beauty was that a satisfactory definition of beauty (in terms of proportion, unity in variety, fitness, or whatever) could not be worked out. The alternative view that beauty is indefinable and transcendental was unacceptable to the British philosophers, who were committed to empiricism. Still another reason for the decline of the theory of beauty was a drift away from theories which conceive of the apparatus of taste as a single sense or a set of special senses specifically related to certain kinds of objects. From about the middle of the eighteenth century, theories began to appear in which the ordinary cognitive and affective faculties plus association constitute the apparatus of taste. These associationistic theories propose that it is possible for almost anything to be beautiful, given the appropriate associations. Thus association provides a means for indefinitely extending the range of things which can be judged beautiful and also renders the traditional way of defining (i.e., by finding something common to all the things denoted by the term to be defined) impossible in the case of beauty. In these theories, beauty becomes an exceedingly diffuse concept which does not serve to distinguish one thing from another. This situation is similar to that of the present-day aesthetic-attitude theories which maintain that anything can be aesthetic if only it is experienced while in the aesthetic attitude.

## Shaftesbury

It is appropriate to begin the discussion of eighteenth-century philosophers by outlining the main features of the thought of the third Earl of Shaftesbury (1671–1713) whose views, although transitional, are of great importance. His diffuse and unsystematic views are transitional because he holds a Platonic theory of beauty but also holds and is the main source of the influential theory of the faculty of taste. These two theories are not logically inconsistent. Nevertheless, although a large number of eighteenth-century British philosophers adopted some version of the faculty-of-taste theory, few if any of these empirically inclined thinkers accepted the Platonic trancendentalism. There is, Shaftesbury thinks, a single faculty of taste which can function either as a moral sense for making judgments about behavior or as a sense of beauty for making judgments about whether or not something possesses that quality. The object of a judgment of beauty is a transcendental one.

Shaftesbury was one of the first eighteenth-century thinkers to focus attention on the sublime, and this is his second influential contribution to aesthetic theory. His interest in the sublime probably derived from his conception of the world as the creation of God; the vastness and incomprehensibility of that creation could only be described as sublime. Even though Shaftesbury distinguished a new aesthetic category, he sought to maintain a unified theory (perhaps unconsciously) by classifying the sublime as one kind of beauty. Both the noting of the sublime and the doctrine of taste are important. The latter was very influential on eighteenth-century thought, and the former began a process which resulted in the formation of the concept of the aesthetic.

Shaftesbury made an even more important contribution when he introduced the notion of *disinterestedness*, which was to become the core of the concept of the aesthetic. Shaftesbury insists on the significance of disinterestedness for morality. That is, in order for an action to have moral merit (not simply good consequences), the person acting must not be motivated solely by selfish motives. Shaftesbury introduced disinterestedness into the theory of beauty in an almost incidental way. The example which is frequently cited as Shaftesbury's demonstration of the necessity of disinterestedness for aesthetic appreciation occurs in a passage in which his main concern is to defend the Platonic thesis that "whatever in nature is beautiful or charming is only a faint shadow of that first beauty."[13] ("That first beauty" is the Platonic Form of Beauty.) Shaftesbury tries to defend his Platonic thesis by constructing an analogy which contrasts the contemplation of beautiful things in the world of sense with the desire to possess them. The analogy is supposed to illuminate the relation between beautiful things ("faint shadows") and the Form of Beauty and show the superiority of the latter. It is debatable whether Shaftesbury's remarks can be called an argument, but it is the example in his analogy which turned out to be important for aesthetic theory, not his argument.

He actually gives four separate examples, all of which contrast the contemplation of beautiful things with the desire to possess them. The example so frequently quoted is "Imagine then, good Philocles, if being taken with the beauty of the ocean, . . . it should come into your head to seek how to command it, and, like some mighty admiral, ride master of the sea, would not the fancy be a little absurd?"[14] Of the four examples, however, this one seems the weakest, because the notion of possessing the ocean is such an odd and vague one. In contrast, the other three examples involve relatively clear notions: the first contrasts the contemplation of a tract of land with the desire to possess the land, the second contrasts the contemplation of a grove of trees with the desire to eat the fruit of the trees, and the third contrasts the contemplation of human beauty with the desire for sexual possession. In fact, the last example most clearly contains the elements which later become important in aesthetic theory.

> . . . certain powerful forms in human kind . . . draw after them a set of eager desires, wishes, and hopes; no way suitable, I must confess, to your rational and refined contemplation of beauty. The proportions of this living architecture, as wonderful as they are, inspire nothing of a studious or contemplative kind.[15]

Since Shaftesbury's time it has been a staple of aesthetic theory that selfish or interested desires, of which the desire for possession is the paradigm, are destructive of aesthetic appreciation. Some theorists have even concluded that selfish or practical desires are wholly incompatible with aesthetic appreciation.

That the contemplation of the qualities of an object is quite a distinct thing from the desire to possess the object must be granted, but the suggestion of Shaftesbury ("no way suitable") and the definite conclusions of some of his followers are both hasty and unfortunate. It is true that the desire for possession might be so compelling and frantic that it would be incompatible with the appreciation of beauty. It is, however, a mistake to generalize from an extreme case. From the obvious fact that ungovernable desire is incompatible with the appreciation of beauty, it does not follow that all desires are in "no way suitable" to appreciation. Shaftesbury's failure to appreciate the importance of degrees of desire is probably rooted in two related conceptions: 1) a puritanism which treats all desire alike and 2) a Platonism which views both the senses and desire as suspect. The fact that for thousands of years people have appreciated the beauty of art which frequently displays "the proportions of this living architecture" and which invites desire does not seem to have occurred to Shaftesbury.

Given his philosophical orientation, it is not surprising that Shaftesbury fails to make the appropriate distinction. Unfortunately, a whole tradition in aesthetics has followed him on this point. The philosophers most influenced in this regard are the aesthetic-attitude theorists, although not every such philosopher follows the extreme disinterestedness line. It should also be noted that Shaftesbury's theory of the disinterested appreciation of beauty is developed in terms of motives: interested or selfish motives (and activity) are thought to undercut appreciation. But many aesthetic-attitude theorists, especially in the present day, have extended the scope of disinterestedness and developed the view that there is a special kind of *perception*—disinterested perception—which is the foundation of aesthetic experience. Disinterested perception will be discussed at some length in Part II.

## Hutcheson

Francis Hutcheson (1694–1746) is perhaps the single best representative of the eighteenth-century British aestheticians. In him the transition to doctrines which characterize this group is complete. There is no trace of Platonic transcendentalism; his theory focuses squarely on the phenomena of sense, and disinterestedness is worked smoothly into his conception of sense.

In Hutcheson's view, not only does the word "beauty" not name a transcendental object, it does not name any object which is seen, heard, or touched. "Beauty" names an "idea rais'd in us";[16] that is, it denotes an object in our private consciousness which is aroused by the perception of certain kinds of external objects. Beauty has become completely subjectivized. Once the experience of beauty is recognizable, an inquiry can be made as to whether there are any features of the objects of perception which regularly trigger the experience of beauty. Hutcheson's answer is *uniformity in variety*. He sometimes refers to uniformity in variety as beauty, but this must be taken as a kind of shorthand because in his theory, strictly speaking, it is the cause of beauty. What Hutcheson meant by "the idea of beauty" might best be rendered in present-day terminology as the feeling of beauty or the beauty feeling.

When Hutcheson speaks of the *sense* of beauty, he means a power or ability to have aroused in a mind the idea or feeling of beauty. Whereas Shaftesbury holds that there is one internal sense with several functions, Hutcheson holds that there are a number of distinct senses which have single functions: a moral sense, a sense of beauty, a sense of grandeur, and so on. But he discusses only the moral sense and the sense of beauty, merely mentioning the other senses. These senses are *internal* senses, which means that their objects are internal to the mind, as contrasted with the external senses such as sight and hearing, whose objects are external. The internal senses are *reactive* in nature rather than perceptual; that is, the internal senses are not a mode of perceiving the world as are vision and hearing.

Following Shaftesbury, Hutcheson tries to refute Thomas Hobbes's psychological theory that all behavior is selfish. His subtle arguments against the self-love theory are better known as they relate to moral philosophy, but his anti-Hobbesian views are also woven into his conception of the sense of beauty. One reason for calling the faculty of beauty a sense, according to Hutcheson, is that awareness of beauty (the idea or feeling of it) is immediate, that is, unmediated by thought. The experience of beauty is like the taste of salt or sugar in this respect. Hutcheson thinks that if the experience of beauty and the approval of something as beautiful are free of thought and calculation, then aesthetic appreciations and approvals cannot be selfish. If I open my eyes and see a red pencil, my awareness of redness is not influenced by any selfish desires, and even if it is greatly in my selfish interest to see green at that moment, there is nothing I can do about it. Hutcheson's theory is designed to make the experience of beauty and judgments about beauty objective by tying them to fundamental, inborn faculties of the human constitution and to make them disinterested by maintaining that these faculties are senses and hence impervious to influence. As Hutcheson puts it, the sense of beauty is passive; that is, it simply reacts in an automatic fashion, and the beauty feeling does not derive from "any knowledge of principles, proportions, causes, or of the usefulness of the object."[17]

## Burke

Edmund Burke (1728–1797) published his book on the sublime and the beautiful[18] shortly after the middle of the eighteenth century. The most important contribution of the book to the historical line being traced here is his full-scale theory of the sublime. He treats the sublime as a category separate from beauty—in fact, he regards the sublime as opposed to beauty. This splitting put an additional strain on the unity in the eighteenth-century theory of beauty.

Burke rejects the theory of special internal senses and tries to make the more ordinary phenomena of pleasure and pain the basis for beauty and the sublime. He distinguishes between positive pleasure and relative pleasure, which he calls "delight." Delight results from the removal of pain or the removal of the anticipation of pain. The pleasure taken in beauty is love (positive pleasure), and this pleasure is generally related to the passions useful for the preservation of society. The pleasure taken in the sublime is delight (relative pleasure), and this being pleased by the removal of pain or threat of pain is generally related to the passions useful for the preservation of the individual. Burke says, "By beauty I mean, that quality, or those qualities in bodies, by which they cause love, or some passion similar to it."[19] Unfortunately, he then defines "love" a few lines further on as "that satisfaction which arises to the mind upon contemplating any thing beautiful."[20] These two passages form a circle and Burke has been criticized for his reasoning. A few lines later, however, he specifies those qualities of bodies—smallness, smoothness, being polished, lines deviating insensibly from "the right line" (right angle), and so on—which trigger love, and perhaps this specification is enough to remove the viciousness from the circle. The sublime is whatever excites delight. The experience of the sublime is induced, for example, by obscure objects and objects of great size. Such objects ordinarily threaten and terrorize us, but if we can contemplate such objects and still be secure, then they are experienced as sublime.

It is worth noting that disinterestedness plays a role in Burke's theory of beauty, and its function is more accurately described by Burke than it is by either Shaftesbury or many of the later aesthetic-attitude theorists.

We shall have a strong desire for a woman of no remarkable beauty; whilst the greatest beauty in men, or in other animals, though it causes love, yet excites nothing at all of desire. Which shews that beauty, and the passion caused by beauty, which I call love, is different from desire, though desire may sometimes operate along with it. . . .[21]

Burke distinguishes between love (the appreciation of beauty) and desire for possession, which is to say that love is disinterested. But he finds no necessary incompatibility between them—they may sometimes "operate" along with one another.

## Gerard, Knight, and Stewart

Several writers deserve mention before going on to Alison, Hume, and Kant. Several points in the theory of Alexander Gerard (1728–1795) deserve mention. He uses the particularly apt phrase "reflex senses" to refer to what earlier philosophers had called "internal senses." "Reflex" makes clear that these senses are reactive in function. Gerard's theory is also something of a high-water mark in the theory of special senses, as he distinguishes seven of them: the senses of novelty, sublimity, beauty, imitation, harmony, ridicule, and virtue. When it seems necessary to postulate this many special faculties—and Gerard's theory was not an isolated example —philosophers become unhappy. Philosophers crave unity, and the very diversity of theories like Gerard's encourages philosophers to turn to new concepts. A remark by Gerard himself indicates why his own and related theories were felt to be unsatisfactory: "There is perhaps no term used in a looser sense than *beauty*, which is applied to almost everything that pleases us."[22] There is little motivation to use a concept as a central one in a theory when the concept is felt to be very vague.

Shortly after the end of the century, Richard Payne Knight

wrote, in a vein which reminds one of present-day emotivist theories, "The word Beauty is a general term of approbation, of the most vague and extensive meaning, applied indiscriminately to almost every thing that is pleasing, . . . whether a material substance, a moral excellence, or an intellectual theorem."[23] A few years later, Dugald Stewart argued that some concepts, including beauty, cannot be defined in the traditional way by specifying something common to all things covered by the concept.[24] Consider objects *A, B, C,* and *D* which fall under the same concept. *A* and *B* may have a quality in common, *B* and *C* may have a quality in common, and *C* and *D* may have a quality in common, but there may not be any important quality which all the objects share. Stewart's point is the same as Ludwig Wittgenstein's famous point that the objects falling under a concept may have only a *family resemblance* to one another.

## Alison

Archibald Alison (1757–1839) published his book on the theory of taste in 1790.[25] His theory may be considered the culmination of the development which was begun at the start of the century by Shaftesbury. His central concern is to map the terrain of the faculty of taste, but he abandons the idea of special internal senses of beauty and the sublime in favor of a very complicated theory involving the ordinary cognitive and affective faculties. He explicitly opposes this view to those of such special-sense philosophers as Hutcheson and Gerard. He also has a fully developed conception of disinterestedness.

The faculty of taste for Alison is "that . . . by which we perceive and enjoy whatever is Beautiful or Sublime in the works of Nature or Art."[26] By "perceive" Alison means something much broader than the present-day meaning of the term. He means something like awareness. Thus he could speak of perceiving (feeling) his own pain. He maintains that human beings are so constituted that certain features of the material world, either objects of nature or of art, cause them to experience what he calls the "emotion of taste." One curious aspect of his theory is that it seems to presuppose the existence of God. In order for an object to evoke the emotion of taste, it must be a sign of or expressive of a quality of mind. For works of art, the mind is the artist's, and for natural objects, the mind is that of the "Divine Artist." What is curious is that what is essentially a psychological theory suddenly presupposes a theological commitment. But this commitment could be avoided by saying that the emotion of taste is evoked when a natural object is *taken to be* a sign of the Divine Artist.

Alison's description of the functioning of the faculty of taste is bewilderingly complex, involving a host of distinct items: objects of taste (works of art and nature), simple emotions, complex emotions, simple pleasures, complex pleasures, trains of thought in the imagination united by association, and a maze of relations among these items. First, when an object of taste is perceived, a simple emotion is produced in the mind. The simple emotion produces a thought (typically an image) in the imagination. This first thought produces a second thought in the imagination and it a third, so that by association a whole *unified* train of thought is produced. Each member of the train of thought also produces a simple emotion, so that in addition to the original simple emotion which started the train of thought, there is a set of simple emotions, the members of which are unified by their relation to the coherent train of thought. This set of simple emotions produces the emotion of taste, which is a complex emotion. In addition, each simple emotion is accompanied by a simple pleasure, and the functioning of the imagination also produces a simple pleasure. This set of simple pleasures constitutes the complex pleasure which accompanies the emotion of taste and which Alison calls "delight." Probably the only way to get a clear idea of this scheme would be for the reader to draw a diagram of it.

Alison's theory is superior to many earlier theories,

Hutcheson's for example, in that it provides a basis for explaining the richness and complexity of the experience of art and nature. It is difficult to explain the experience of a great deal of art in terms of uniformity in variety, and thus Hutcheson's view has been criticized as sterile and even vacuous. Alison's theory is so oriented toward complexity that he denies that simple sense qualities (unless taken as signs of something) can be objects of taste. "The smell of a rose, the color of scarlet, the taste of a pineapple, when spoken of merely as qualities, and abstracted from the objects in which they are found, are said to produce agreeable Sensations, but not agreeable Emotions."[27] No emotions, no objects of taste. Alison's argument may be one source of the persistent prejudice against simple sense qualities as "not aesthetic."

Alison's commitment to disinterestedness is evident when he considers the state of mind "most favorable to the emotion of taste." This occurs when "attention is so little occupied by any private or particular object of thought, as to leave us open to all the impressions which the objects that are before us can produce. It is upon the vacant and the unemployed, accordingly, that the objects of taste make the strongest impression."[28] "The husbandman" and "the man of business" are oblivious to the beauty of, say, some aspect of nature because they are interested in profiting from it, and "the philosopher" is oblivious because he is lost in thought. Because Alison here speaks of the conditions *"most* favorable to the emotion of taste," it does not follow that interest is incompatible with the emotion of taste. Still, the drift of his remarks gives aid and comfort to those who wish to separate the aesthetic from considerations of interest—the useful, the personal, and so on. In fact, Alison concludes that criticism destroys appreciation because it considers art in relation to rules or compares it to other art. That criticism is incompatible with appreciation is an unfortunate and persistent prejudice which results from pressing the significance of disinterestedness too far.

## Hume

It is out of chronological order to discuss Hume after Alison because Hume's "Of the Standard of Taste"[29] was published in the middle of the eighteenth century. I do so, however, because Hume's formulation of what might be called "the British view" provides the strongest possible contrast with the theory of the German philosopher Kant, whose views are to be discussed next. Hume's account of the nature of taste does not add anything new to *the content* of the British view—it is basically Hutchesonian in flavor—but Hume has a much deeper understanding of the philosophical issues involved in theorizing about taste than do the aestheticians discussed thus far. For example, Hume makes explicit that he assumes, as did the other British aestheticians, that the inquiry into the nature of taste is an empirical investigation of certain aspects of human nature.

"Of the Standard of Taste," which is a short essay, is Hume's only work on the problem of taste. He begins the essay by admitting that there is a great variation and disagreement among men on questions of taste. The task of the essay is to show that these disagreements are due to the accidental features of the circumstances in which men find themselves. Hume first states the skeptical view that it is impossible to dispute taste and then claims that such a view entails the absurd consequent that we cannot rate any work above any other.

> Whoever would assert an equality of genius and elegance between Ogilby and Milton, or Bunyan and Addison, would be thought to defend no less an extravagance, than if he had maintained a mole-hill to be as high as Teneriffe, or a pond as extensive as the ocean.[30]

He concludes that the skeptical view is false.

Hume first rejects reasoning *a priori* as the source of what he calls "the rules of composition" (the standard of taste). This view he shares with the other British aestheticians we have discussed, except Shaftesbury. He is denying that we rationally intuit beauty or the rules which govern it. He affirms that the foundation of the rules of composition is *experience*. The rules of composition are "but general observations, concerning what has been universally found to please in all countries and in all ages."[31] His claim is then that the normative question of what it is correct to call beautiful can be solved by a comprehensive empirical survey of the taste of men. It is this feature of the British view which contrasts sharply with Kant's theory.

But even if Hume conceives of himself as sketching the outlines of an empirical investigation, he states that not every case of a man being pleased is to count as evidence for the generalizations which are the rules of composition. Certain kinds of cases must be discounted, and Hume makes a careful attempt to spell out the conditions under which a proper inquiry can be made.

> When we would make an experiment of this nature, and would try the force of any beauty or deformity, we must choose with care a proper time and place, and bring the fancy to a suitable situation and disposition. A perfect serenity of mind, a recollection of thought, a due attention to the object; if any of these circumstances be wanting, our experiment will be fallacious, and we shall be unable to judge of the catholic and universal beauty.[32]

These conditions must be met in order to rule out cases of being pleased which are the result of the caprices of fashion and the mistakes of ignorance and envy. In addition to these considerations, there is the alleged fact that what Hume here calls "mental taste" is more acute in some persons than in others. Just as some persons can discriminate more accurately in the case of "bodily taste"—for example, in distinguishing the subtle qualities of wine—some persons are better in discriminating those qualities which trigger the faculty of taste. Only those persons who possess what Hume calls "delicacy of taste" are fit subjects for his *experiment*.

Hume's methodological considerations have now been spelled out. His substantive, although very abstract, conclusion is well stated in the following quotation:

> Though it be certain, that beauty and deformity, more than sweet and bitter, are not qualities in objects, but belong entirely to the sentiment, internal or external; it must be allowed, that there are certain qualities in objects, which are fitted by nature to produce those particular feelings.[33]

Notice that beauty and its opposite, deformity, are not *in objects* but are *feelings*. The feelings, however, are not just feelings but are feelings linked by the nature of our human constitution to "certain qualities in objects." Thus it is possible to have objective judgments about beauty and deformity in the sense that universal agreement among normal subjects is possible. Notice also that Hume, unlike his fellow British aestheticians, does not specify what the "certain qualities in objects" are.

After having developed an objective theory of taste based on certain alleged stabilities in human nature, at the end of his essay Hume allows for certain acceptable variations of taste due to age and temperament. Young men prefer "amorous and tender images," but older men prefer "wise philosophical reflections." "Mirth or passion, sentiment or reflection; which ever of these most predominates in our temper, it gives us a peculiar sympathy with the writer who resembles us."[34] In such cases no standard of taste is available to rate one preference better than the other. Is Hume consistent in allowing such variation? Probably so, for the diversity has its origin in the factors of age and temperament, factors which cannot be ruled out by the conditions of Hume's experiment and which are not due to the inability to discriminate. Is, however, Hume's experimental approach the right method? Kant certainly does not think so.

## Kant

The major roadblock to understanding the theory of taste presented by German philosopher Immanuel Kant (1724–1804) is that it is part of a formidable philosophical system. His statement of the theory bristles with technical terms and is organized according to a complex scheme worked out earlier for his theory of knowledge. Insofar as it is possible, the technical aspects of his system are avoided here. Only his theory of beauty will be discussed; his theory of the sublime is omitted. Kant consciously uses the work of the thinkers already discussed and is clearly within the tradition of the philosophy of taste.

In order to understand Kant's theory of beauty, it is necessary to have some idea of his philosophical system, which differs radically from that of Hume and the empiricist British aestheticians. Hume, for example, held that knowledge derives wholly from experience and that consequently we cannot be certain of anything. Kant tried to develop a system which would show how it is possible for us to have some knowledge which is certain.[35] In brief, Kant maintains that the mind itself contributes the structure that our experience has and that for this reason we can have certain knowledge. For example, we know that every event will have a cause because the mind structures the events of our experience into a causal network. This difference between Kant's philosophy and that of the empiricists shows up in their respective philosophies of taste. The empiricists conceived of the philosophy of taste as an empirical inquiry the object of which is to arrive at psychological generalizations about human nature. Kant conceives of the philosophy of taste as an inquiry into the *a priori* foundations of knowledge which will show why judgments of beauty are universal and necessary.[36]

Kant uses the term "aesthetic" in a very broad sense to include not only judgments of beauty and the sublime but also judgments about pleasure in general. For Kant, all aesthetic judgments focus on pleasure, which is a property of the experiencing subject rather than of the objective world. Such judgments are *subjective* because pleasure does not play a role in the cognition of the objective world external to the subject. This doctrine reflects Hutcheson's view that beauty is an "idea rais'd in us." But if judgments of beauty are subjective, Kant also thinks that they are stable and universal in a way that other pleasures are not. That is, he seeks a theory which will show that although the pleasure felt in the taste of, say, chocolate or anchovies is merely personal, the pleasure felt with beauty is universal and necessary. Kant divides the discussion of his theory of beauty into four parts, each of which treats a major concept. These concepts are 1) disinterestedness, 2) universality, 3) the form of purpose, and 4) necessity. The theory may be summarized in a sentence: A judgment of beauty is a disinterested, universal, and necessary judgment concerning the pleasure which everyone *ought* to derive from the experience of form.

Kant characterizes interest in terms of desire and real existence; that is, to have an interest in something is at least to have a desire that that thing actually exist or at least to have a desire concerning its existence. An interest may, of course, be either self-regarding or altruistic. Kant argues, following the British philosophers, that judgments of beauty are disinterested; that is, they are indifferent to the real existence of their objects. Care should be taken to note that Kant does not say that a person who makes a judgment of beauty is indifferent to the existence of the object of the judgment, but simply that the judgment of beauty is independent of the interest in real existence. Once a person correctly makes a judgment of beauty, then no doubt he will typically assume an interest in the existence of the object which is responsible for his experience, but this is a second and different judgment. One of Shaftesbury's examples can be used to illustrate the point. If I appreciate the qualities of fruit in the way which involves a judgment of beauty, my appreciation and my judgment are directed toward the visual qualities of the object I am aware of and not toward the existence of the object which makes that awareness possible.

Kant discusses universality and necessity at different times, but they will be treated together here. He asserts that the universality of judgments of beauty is deducible from their disinterested nature. If a person is pleased with something in a disinterested way, then the pleasure cannot derive from anything personal and peculiar to the person. Interest springs from individual inclinations, but this is just what disinterestedness rules out. Consequently, if disinterested pleasure is possible, then it must derive from what is common to all mankind and not from interests which are peculiar to some persons only. When we utter judgments of taste, we speak, Kant says, "with a universal voice." But he maintains that aesthetic judgments ("This rose in beautiful") are subjective, which means that "beautiful" is not a concept as, for example, "red" is. When one says that a rose is red, the concept "red" is being applied to *this rose* and the concept refers to an objective feature of the world. Any normal man can look at the rose and see that it is red, and this confers universality on the statement, "This rose is red." But how can this be done when "beautiful" does not refer to something objective? Kant falls back on the familiar notion of the faculty of taste, not the special-sense version but the version in which ordinary cognitive faculties function in an unusual way. First, the cognitive faculties are common to all men and in their ordinary employment produce universally valid judgments about the objective world. In aesthetic appreciation, rather than doing their usual *work,* the cognitive faculties of sensory awareness and the understanding (the faculty of concepts) engage in *free play*. This free play exhibits the harmonious relation of the cognitive faculties and results in the pleasure felt in aesthetic appreciation. The pleasure is universally valid because it depends solely on universal faculties.

Judgments of beauty, an addition to their universality, have a necessity. This necessity is justified by Kant in a way similar to that used to justify the universality of judgments of taste. When we say that something is beautiful, we are, Kant thinks, making a demand that everyone agree with us. He states that of course not everyone *will* agree with us. The reason that we make such a demand is that we are talking about something causing a pleasure which derives from faculties common to all men. Thus, if something gives one person pleasure as the result of the free play of the cognitive faculties (which all men share), it ought to give any man pleasure. In other words, the thing ought *necessarily* to give pleasure to every man. Kant, however, denies that we can derive general rules of beauty, as Hume wishes to do. Every judgment of taste is a *singular* judgment, and no general rule can be formulated from the whole set of judgments. If Kant's view is correct, it is easy enough to see why all men *ought* to agree, but it does not tell us how we can get such agreement. Perhaps if the kinds of conditions that Hume specifies for his experiments were met, then we would get agreement.

Disinterestedness, universality, and necessity are primarily involved with the experiencing subject. The fourth concept that Kant discusses—the form of purpose—focuses on the object of the appreciation. Kant is raising the point which Hutcheson tried to make by talking about uniformity in variety. Each of the philosophers of taste tries, in addition to giving his own description of the faculty of taste, to specify exactly what feature or features of the objective world it is that triggers that faculty. Like Hutcheson, Kant focuses on *formal* relations as the stimulus of the beauty experience. Unlike Hutcheson, for reasons which are at best difficult to make clear, Kant wishes to work the notion of purpose into his theory at this point. He must be careful in doing this, however, because the recognition that something has a purpose involves applying a concept, which would make the judgment of taste objective rather than subjective and would take that judgment past immediately experienced qualities. Consequently, he asserts that it is recognition of the *form* of purpose, not recognition of the purpose itself, which evokes the beauty experience. The form of a work of art—for example, the design of a painting or the compositional structure of a musical piece—is the result of purposive activity of a human agent. The forms of nature are, or can be taken to be, the result of purposive activity of God. Judgments of taste focus on these forms themselves without considering them in relation to the purpose they realize. Kant denies that color is beautiful; he says it is agreeable. The agreeable pleasure of color may be enjoyed along with pleasure taken in form, but the two are distinct. Only form is beautiful. Men may disagree about what colors they find pleasant without raising any problem, but they ought to agree about form. Of course, forms are built up out of colored elements, but the forms are distinguishable from their elements. Similar considerations hold for nonvisual forms and their elements.

## Summary

With Kant, the theory of the faculty of taste in its various versions has pretty well run its course. By his time, philosophers had largely lost their taste for faculties as a way of solving philosophical problems. When faculties were no longer available to furnish a kind of minimal unity to the fragmented elements of the field, the concept of the aesthetic seized the imagination of philosophers and they began to organize their theories around it instead. Each of the philosophies of taste discussed here subjectivized beauty, but only partially; for each claimed that some specific feature of the *objective* world triggered the faculty of taste. Thus each theory made an attempt to anchor itself to some objective aspect of the world. The following list summarizes this feature of each theory.

| | |
|---|---|
| Shaftesbury | the Form of Beauty |
| Hutcheson | uniformity in variety |
| Burke | smallness, smoothness, etc. |
| Alison | a sign of a quality of mind |
| Hume | certain unspecified qualities |
| Kant | the form of purpose |

As the philosophy-of-taste approach was abandoned, "aesthetic" theories began to take hold. These theories are totally subjectivized. The following quotation from the work of the nineteenth-century German philosopher Arthur Schopenhauer is a good illustration of an aesthetic theory.

> When we say that a thing is *beautiful,* we thereby assert that it is an object of our aesthetic contemplation, . . . it means that the sight of the thing makes us *objective,* that is to say, that in contemplating it we are no longer conscious of ourselves as individuals, but as pure will-less subjects of knowledge. . . .[37]

This theory is totally subjectivized in that a thing is said to be beautiful because it is an object of our aesthetic contemplation. No specific objective character is required for something to be beautiful; an object's beauty is *imposed* on it as the result of being the object of some person's aesthetic consciousness. Anything can become beautiful if aesthetic consciousness is turned on it. Theories of aesthetic consciousness in one form or another have continued to be developed and defended up to the present, and in Part II several present-day developments from Schopenhauer's theory will be examined.

As I have thus far presented matters, it may appear that there was a radical break between eighthteenth-century theories of taste and nineteenth-century aesthetic theories. A close consideration of Kant's concept of form as the thing which triggers the faculty of taste, however, reveals that his theory has elements of both the earlier and later theories. Hence Kant's aesthetics can be seen as the link between the theories of the two centuries. In the summary table given above, the form of purpose is listed as Kant's answer to what was a set question for the theory of taste: "What feature of the world evokes aesthetic pleasure?" Kant's answer differs in an important way from that of the other philosophers listed. In the case of each of the other philosophers, the specified feature is conceived to be an aspect of the world which is entirely independent of the experiencing subject. Form, however, according to Kant's general philosophical view, is the contribution of the subject's mind. In other words, the

forms that the objects of our experience have are imposed by
the structuring mind. Consequently, the thing which triggers
the faculty of taste is itself wholly mental in character. This
in effect means that the mind triggers itself, and it is not so
far from saying this to saying with Schopenhauer that the
aesthetic consciousness imposes beauty on objects. Without
trying to work out the details of the relations between Kant's
and Schopenhauer's views, it may be seen that there is continuity here.

The significance of the eighteenth century for aesthetics
may be roughly summarized as follows. Before the eighteenth
century, *beauty* was a central concept; during the century,
it was replaced by the concept of *taste;* by the end of the
century, the concept of taste had been exhausted and the way
was open for the concept of *the aesthetic.*

I turn now to the other central strain in the history of
aesthetics, the philosophy of art.

---

## Chapter 3.  The Theory of Art

---

### Introductory Remarks

THE FIRST PART of this chapter will consist of a discussion of
the imitation theory of art advanced by Plato and Aristotle,
together with a discussion of their theories of the origin of
art and of the effect of art on people. The only other theory
of art which will be discussed in this chapter is expressionism, a nineteenth-century view which was the first theory to
challenge the dominance of the imitation theory. In the
period between Plato and the nineteenth century, debate
over the theory of art took place within the imitation theory

and was concerned with the proper objects to be imitated. Present-day theories of art will be discussed in Part III.

The imitation theory of Plato and Aristotle focuses attention on the objective properties of the work of art. It may be said that this theory of art is *object-centered*. Plato also held an emotionalistic theory about the origin and effect of art. The development of the expressionist theory of art in the nineteenth century can be thought of as a conversion of the emotionalistic theory of the origin and effect of art into a theory of art itself. What Plato had kept separate as two theories was collapsed by the expressionists into one. Expressionism shifts attention away from the work of art toward the artist; this theory is *artist-centered*.

Although both Plato and Aristotle hold the imitation theory of art, they have radically different views about how art affects people. It should also be noted that Plato's imitation theory is rather hostile to art, whereas Aristotle's version is friendly to art.

## Plato

That art is imitation was no doubt a popularly held view of Plato's time. What Plato does is to work this conception into his philosophical theory of the Forms, an adaptation which produces a two-level theory of imitation. In the *Republic*[38] Plato says that an artisan who makes furniture, say, a chair, imitates the Form of Chairness and an artist who paints a picture of the chair imitates the chair. There are, then, two levels of imitation. Of course, when an artist paints a picture of a natural object, i.e., a nonartifact, there are still two levels of imitation. Plato's contention is that there are the Forms, the objects in the world of sense which imitate the Forms, and presentations made by artists which imitate the objects of the world of sense. Plato compares paintings with mirror images, suggesting that paintings are only appearances and thereby "untrue." (Actually, paintings should be called appearances of appearances in Platonic theory, since objects of the world of sense are appearances of the Forms.) Plato's characterization of paintings as untrue appearances may be the origin of the view that art is illusion, a view held by a number of present-day theorists.

Plato's first quarrel with art, and the one which flows directly from his conception of art, is that since it is a twice-removed imitation of reality, it cannot be a good source of knowledge. Plato thus places art in competition with such disciplines as mathematics and science as a source of knowledge. He is especially concerned to press this contention in connection with the art of poetry, and with some point. The poetry of Homer and other poets was considered by many Greeks to be authoritative not only as a source of knowledge concerning horsemanship, the making of war, and other such technical matters, but also as a source of moral knowledge. Plato maintains that only a philosopher can be the source of moral knowledge and that only specialists in such areas as horsemanship are accurate guides in such technical matters. When poets speak of chariot driving, making war, or noble action, they only pretend to know and hence are false guides. Plato's first quarrel with art is that art is doubly unreal and hence is an especially inferior product and a poor guide for conduct.

Plato's second quarrel with art concerns its alleged bad effect on people, both because it sometimes presents unsuitable examples of conduct and because of its emotional nature. The former problem can be dealt with by censorship, and Plato advocates a very severe censorship in the ideal state. But the emotional nature of art, which derives from its irrational source, is more difficult to deal with and is perhaps impossible to eradicate. In the dialogue entitled *Ion*,[39] in a discussion with the rhapsode Ion, Socrates sets forth a theory which purports to explain how poetry is created and how it affects spectators. The main point is that the process is an irrational one and that all the human beings involved with poetry are "out of their minds." The poet creates a poem not by a rational procedure but by being inspired by a god.

When a rhapsode such as Ion performs, he is inspired by the poem and the spectator is inspired by the rhapsode. Socrates uses the analogy of a magnet and a set of iron rings: an iron ring will cling to a magnet, a second iron ring will cling to the first iron ring, and so on until there is a chain of rings. Only the first ring touches the magnet, but the magnet's power passes through the whole chain and sustains it. Analogously, the god through his inspiration sustains the chain of poet, rhapsode, and spectator. None of the human beings in the chain *knows* what he is doing, each is being manipulated by forces outside himself. A spectator may weep or appear panic-stricken when listening to a rhapsode or watching a play. Poetry "waters the passions" rather than instructs reason, and Plato has great fear of its effects on spectators. He believes that this feeding of the passions will produce bad citizens. In a dialogue entitled *Phaedrus*,[40] he seems to take a more sympathetic view of inspiration when he says that a poet possessed by the muses and in a frenzy will produce better poetry than a sane man who tries to write poetry with the help of technical skill, i.e., rationally. Thus Plato's second quarrel with art is somewhat ambivalent. It should be noted that when Plato talks about inspiration he speaks only of poetry, and he may have wished to restrict the theory to the creation of poetry. That is, he may not have been setting forth a general theory about the creation of all art.

## Aristotle

Plato's interest in art is derivative and arises within the context of an attempt to deal with problems such as the place of the artist in the ideal state. Aristotle, however, takes a direct interest in art or rather in the various species of art such as tragedy and comedy. Either Aristotle did not devote a work to the general topic of art or it has not survived. There are a number of remarks about art in his various works, but his main contribution to aesthetics is his *Poetics,* which is concerned with three species of art: tragedy, comedy, and epic poetry. Despite these differences from Plato, it is clear that Aristotle agrees with Plato that art is imitation. However, since Aristotle holds that the Forms are not separate from the world of sense, he has no hostility toward the world of sense as such and consequently no hostility toward art which imitates the world of sense. In fact, Aristotle's general philosophical position intrudes very little on his poetic theory, or perhaps it should be said that his general philosophic position allows him to base his poetic theory on an analysis of actual tragedies, comedies, and epics. One of the impressive things about the *Poetics*[41] is the wealth of information it contains about the history of the art forms being discussed, about technical aspects of plays and of the theater.

The *Poetics* is a theory of literature, or more specifically of literature as it existed in Greek times. Given that literature is imitation, Aristotle's first problem is to distinguish the various species of literature from one another and ultimately give definitions for the species. In order to do this, he distinguishes three aspects of imitation: medium of imitation, object of imitation, and manner of imitation. As the media of imitation, he cites rhythm, language, and tone. But media alone are not sufficient to sort out poetry from prose; for example, both Homer who was a poet and Empedocles who was a philosopher wrote in verse. The object of imitation is *men acting,* and this aspect will distinguish, for example, comedy (which imitates the action of base men) from tragedy (which imitates the action of noble men) . Manner of imitation involves the question of whether the story is told by narration or direct discourse or both, or by having actors act it out. Aristotle thinks that these distinctions will be useful in distinguishing and defining the various literary genre.

Having made these initial distinctions, Aristotle then discusses the origin and history of tragedy, comedy, and epic poetry. He then gives his famous definition of tragedy and specifies the six elements of tragedy—plot, character, language, thought, spectacle, and music. The remaining four-fifths of the *Poetics* is devoted to a detailed analysis of the elements of tragedy with a little space given to the epic and comedy. The great bulk of this analysis is a discussion of plot: the size and unity of plot, the relation of plot to history and legend, types of plot, plot reversals, the best kinds of plots and defective plots, and so on. Aristotle's definition of tragedy is as follows:

> Tragedy, then, is the imitation of a good action, which is complete and of a certain length, by means of language made pleasing for each part separately; it relies in its various elements not on narrative but on acting; through pity and fear it achieves the purgation (catharsis) of such emotions.[42]

Notice that Aristotle builds into his definition his general theory of art (imitation) and his three initial distinctions: object of imitation (good action), medium of imitation (language made pleasing), and manner of imitation (acting). But also notice that he places in his definition his doctrine of *catharsis*. This means that he builds into his definition a subjective element involving the emotions of spectators along with the large number of objective elements which refer to aspects of tragedies themselves. His theory of tragedy, therefore, has a kinship to some later expressionist theories of art.

The theory of catharsis is probably Aristotle's attempt to combat Plato's suspicions that art, or at least tragedy, leaves the spectator in an emotionally agitated and dangerous frame of mind. According to Aristotle, tragedy purges the spectator of pity and fear, and he leaves the theater free of such emotions. Aristotle apparently takes seriously Plato's contention that poetry, of which tragedy is a species, is inherently bound up with emotion, but he develops a theory that tragedy does not have bad effects. Unfortunately, Aristotle has very little to say about emotion in the *Poetics*. There is not even a discussion of catharsis in the *Poetics* as it has come down to us, and the interpretation of catharsis as a therapeutic effect on spectators is based upon a passage in Aristotle's *Politics*.[43]

The last clause of the definition of tragedy stipulates that the action imitated must be pitiful and fearful, and this condition dictates the conclusions which Aristotle draws much later in the *Poetics* about the nature of the tragic hero. The tragic hero has two essential characteristics: 1) he must be a man like us, with regard to virtue, who goes from good to bad fortune, and 2) his bad fortune must result from an error (the tragic flaw). In order for the events of the play to be *fearful* to us, bad fortune must befall someone like us, that is, someone with whom we can identify. In order for the events of the play to be *pitiful*, bad fortune must not befall a good man (that would be repulsive) or a bad man (he would deserve what he got); through an error, it must befall a man who is neither good nor bad. There are perhaps some problems of consistency or at least of interpretation to be worked out among the definition of tragedy, the characterization of the tragic hero, and other of Aristotle's remarks about the characters in tragedy, but that cannot be attempted here.

## The Expression Theory of Art

It was not until shortly before the beginning of the nineteenth century that the imitation theory of art was called into question. During the nineteenth century, the theory that art, and especially literature, is the expression of the emotion of the artist came to be the dominant view, and the imitation theory went into an extended period of withering away. A theory of art does not spring up in an intellectual vacuum. The fact that art in Greece typically had a representative function was converted into a *theory* of art by attaching it to the theory of the Forms. The rise of the expression theory of art is related to Romanticism, an important intellectual and philosophical development of the eighteenth and nineteenth centuries.

The philosophical doctrines which underlie Romanticism are mainly those of Fichte, Schelling, Schopenhauer,
and Nietzsche. These philosophers developed lines of
thought which have their origins in Kant's theory of knowledge. Kant distinguishes between 1) the empirical world of
nature, which is the object of scientific knowledge, and 2)
the noumenal world, which in some sense lies behind the
world of sense and of which we cannot know anything (knowledge being restricted to the empirical world). In part, the
world of experience has the nature it has because of the structure which is impressed upon it by the structure of the mind.
The world of noumena, or things-in-themselves, undistorted
by the structures of the human mind and lying mysteriously
behind the sensuous world, fascinated many philosophers and
men of letters in the nineteenth century. As far as philosophical theory is concerned, Romanticism may be thought
of as a reaction against empiricist philosophy and the scientific mentality and as an attempt to reach behind the sensuous screen of ordinary knowledge to something thought to be
vital and important. A strong aura of religion and mysticism
hovers around Romanticism.

When philosophical Romanticism was applied to the
world of art, it generated a new role for the artist and a new
interest in artistic creation. The artist was conceived to be
a means of getting in touch with vital sources and of attaining a kind of knowledge which science could not give, and
artistic creation was identified or at least associated with the
release of emotion. In this context, emotion assumes an
importance it had not previously had; it is somehow involved
in attaining a superior kind of knowledge. And art becomes
the vehicle of this knowledge and a competitor of science.
This new role for the artist is pointed up by the following
passage from Nietzsche's *Will to Power.*

Our aesthetics have hitherto been women's aesthetics, inas-
much as they have only formulated the experiences of what
is beautiful, from the point of view of the receivers in art.
In the whole of philosophy hitherto the artist has been
lacking.[44]

Nietzsche's statement is something of an exaggeration because Plato's theory of artistic creation resembles in certain respects the Romantic conception.

In addition to these philosophical developments, there seems to have been at the time a heightened appreciation of Dionysian qualities in art (vigor, intensity, elation) and a decreased interest in Apollonian qualities (calmness, order). Out of this intellectual milieu emerged the expression theory of art: art is the expression of the emotion of its creator (the artist). Most versions of the expression theory follow this two-term formula: one term stipulates the expression of emotion, the other stipulates *by* the artist. For example, Eugène Véron writes late in the nineteenth century,

> Art is the manifestation of emotion, obtaining external interpretation, now by expressive arrangement of line, form or color, now by a series of gestures, sounds, or words governed by particular rhythmic cadence.[45]

Alexander Smith (?–1851), writing in 1835, defines poetry by contrasting it with prose.

> The essential distinction between poetry and prose is this: —prose is the language of *intelligence,* poetry of *emotion.* In prose, we communicate our *knowledge* of the objects of sense or thought—in poetry, we express how these objects affect us.[46]

Leo Tolstoy (1828–1910) holds a three-term version of the expression theory which brings reference to spectators, readers, and the like into the definition of art.

> Art is a human activity consisting in this, that one man consciously, by means of certain external signs, hands on to others feelings he has lived through, and that other people are infected by these feelings and also experience them.[47]

The expression theory of art can be seen as an attempt to accomplish a number of things. First, it is an attempt to reestablish for art a central place in Western culture. By the nineteenth century the increasing role of science and the consequent expansion of technology and industrialization had greatly reduced the relative role and status of art in the life of the culture. The expression theory tries to show that art can also do something important for people. And if this is so, the role of the artist takes on a significance which it had not previously had. Second, the expression theory is an attempt to relate art to the lives of people. Emotion is something everyone is capable of experiencing, and that it is important is clear to everyone. Third, and the last thing to be mentioned here, the theory is an attempt to account for the emotional qualities of art and the way in which art moves people. The imitation theory seems adequate to explain why a work which represents (imitates) an emotional event, say, the Crucifixion, has an emotional impact on people. However, art which is not representative in any apparent way, say, instrumental music or nonobjective painting, can also be very moving. Music, by the way, plays a large role in the thought of the romantic philosophers, and the great development of music in the centuries just prior to the nineteenth century provided a strong motive for rejecting the imitation theory and thereby paved the way for the expression theory. The expressive power of music seemed to be positive support for the theory.

## What Is a Theory of Art?

What is a philosopher supposed to be doing when he works out a theory or definition of art? According to the traditional approach to definition, a philosopher would have to specify the necessary and sufficient conditions needed for something to be a work of art. A necessary condition for being an $X$ is a characteristic which any object must have in order to be an $X$. A sufficient condition of an $X$ is a characteristic which, if an object has that characteristic, it is an $X$. For example, consider the Greek definition of man as a rational animal. According to this definition, rationality and animality are each *individually* necessary for something to be a man and rationality and animality are *jointly* sufficient for something to be a man.

Both the imitation and the expression theories of art are so simple that it is perhaps not surprising that both theories appear to fall when judged as traditional definitions. At the level of necessary condition, it is perhaps impossible to show that every work of art imitates; for example, much music and, by definition, nonobjective painting do not imitate. Similarly, not every work of art seems to express emotion; for example, some works consist wholly of formal designs.

The heroic way to defend either of these theories as at least necessary conditions is to say that each theory specifies a characteristic which is an essence of art and that any object which fails to have that characteristic just is not art. The embarrassing consequence of this defense is that one is left with a large class of objects, the members of which everyone (except the defender) calls "art" and treats as if they were art, but which the defender insists are not art. This raises the general philosophical question of how disputes about the adequacy of definition are to be settled, but there is not the space to discuss that problem here.

It may be that a definition of art cannot be given; the concept of art may be too rich and complicated to be captured in the traditional manner. This problem will be discussed in Part III. But if the imitation and expression definitions are inadequate as theories of art, they clearly do say something important about some aspects of some works of art. That a certain work of art is imitative is sometimes the most important feature of that work, and if the imitative aspect of a work is not its *most* important feature, it may still be an important one. Similarly, the emotional content of art is frequently of great significance. (Whether or not it is significant that the emotional content is *someone's expression* is a question that requires a detailed inquiry.) Because of the obvious pertinence of both theories to certain elements in works of art, neither the imitation nor the expression theory should simply be dismissed. Perhaps both may be thought of as theories of *aspects* of art, that is, theories which have a limited application within the class of art and which point to significant and widely pervasive features in art.

While on the subject of the theory of art, I should point out that the term "art" or "work of art" is used in at least two senses: a classificatory sense and an evaluative sense. The first sense concerns the question of whether or not a given object is to be classified as a work of art. The classification of something as a work of art, however, does not determine that the thing is a *good* work of art. The fact that an animal is correctly classified as a horse does not mean that it is a good horse. However, "work of art" is sometimes used to make a positive evaluation of something. A painting or waterfall may be praised by saying that it is a work of art. It is easy to see that "This painting is a work of art" is an evaluation and not a classification because the first two words in the sentence ("This painting") alone presuppose that the object being referred to must be classified as a work of art. It is important not to confuse these two senses.

---

## Chapter 4. Aesthetics Today

---

IN THIS SECTION a brief sketch of the main areas of contemporary aesthetics will be attempted. This outline may be useful to the reader in understanding the chapters which follow and in organizing his thoughts when he reads books and articles on aesthetics.

The subject matter of aesthetics has been presented here divided into two areas: 1) the philosophy of the aesthetic, which replaced the philosophy of beauty, and 2) the philosophy of art. Recent developments in general philosophy and in the thought of art critics (mostly literary) have produced what may be either a third area in aesthetics or a competitor to replace the theory of the aesthetic as one of the two areas in aesthetics. This new development is called "the philosophy of criticism," or "metacriticism," and it is conceived of as a philosophical activity which analyzes and clarifies the basic concepts which art critics use when they describe, interpret, or evaluate particular works of art. The development in philosophy which led to metacriticism in aesthetics was the widespread influence of analytic, linguistic philosophy, which conceives of philosophy as a second-order activity taking as its subject matter the language of some first-order activity. For example, ethics on this view is the activity of analyzing the basic concepts of the language used in moral activity, i.e., language used in blaming, praising, judging goodness, and so on. The relevant development in art criticism was the renewed emphasis by such critics as I. A. Richards and the school of critics known as the New Critics[48] on the importance of focusing critical attention on the works themselves rather than on the biography of the artist and the like. The rise of the New Criticism was important to the development of metacriticism because it is the concepts used by the New Critics in describing, interpreting, and evaluating works of art which the metacritics (the philosophers) took to be their subject matter. Of course, the concepts of any linguistic activity can become the subject matter of the analytic philosopher. Examples of the concepts which an art critic might use are representation ("The painting is a representation of London Bridge"), the intention of the artist ("The poem is a good one because the poet succeeded in realizing his intention"), or form ("This music has a sonata form").

Roughly speaking, the present-day inheritors of the theory of the aesthetic are the philosophers who use and defend the notion of the aesthetic attitude. Such philosophers maintain that there is an identifiable aesthetic attitude and that any object, artifactual or natural, toward which a person takes the aesthetic attitude can become an aesthetic object. An aesthetic object is the focus or cause of aesthetic experience

# THE DOMAIN OF AESTHETICS

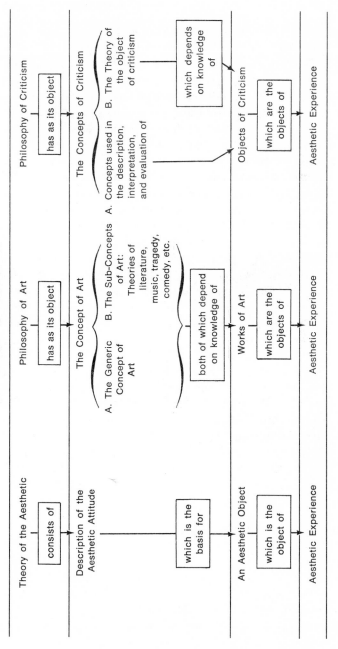

Theory of the Aesthetic

consists of

Description of the Aesthetic Attitude

which is the basis for

An Aesthetic Object

which is the object of

Aesthetic Experience

Philosophy of Art

has as its object

The Concept of Art

A. The Generic Concept of Art

B. The Sub-Concepts of Art: Theories of literature, music, tragedy, comedy, etc.

both of which depend on knowledge of

Works of Art

which are the objects of

Aesthetic Experience

Philosophy of Criticism

has as its object

The Concepts of Criticism

A. Concepts used in the description, interpretation, and evaluation of

B. The Theory of the object of criticism

which depends on knowledge of

Objects of Criticism

which are the objects of

Aesthetic Experience

and therefore the proper object of attention, appreciation, and criticism. There is nothing in metacriticism, i.e., the analysis of the concepts of criticism, which actually contradicts the theory of the aesthetic attitude. In fact, Jerome Stolnitz, who is one of the most prominent attitude theorists, conceives of aesthetics and presents it in his book[49] as the theory of the aesthetic attitude plus metacriticism. However, Monroe Beardsley, who is the foremost defender of metacriticism, develops his complete theory without using the notion of the aesthetic attitude.[50] Others have explicitly argued that the notion of the aesthetic attitude is untenable.[51] The attitude theory will be examined in detail in Part II.

The diagram presented here will perhaps help make the organization of present-day aesthetics clearer. If the diagram is not completely clear to the reader at first glance, it is hoped that it will be when he has finished the book. One comment concerning the diagram is in order. Art and its subconcepts are concepts which critics use, and for that reason it might be thought that they are simply concepts of criticism and that the philosophy of art is subsumable under the philosophy of criticism. But philosophers have had a *direct* interest in the concept of art since the time of Plato, long before the rise of the idea of the philosophy of criticism. If this argument is unconvincing, the independence of the two areas is demonstrated by the fact that some of the essential aspects of works of art are not things of the sort to which criticism can be addressed. This point will be argued in Parts II and III.

# PART II

---

# The Aesthetic: Attitude and Object

---

PART I was concerned with the history of the organizing strains of aesthetics. The remaining chapters of the book are concerned with the problems of present-day aesthetics. The discussion of the first of the organizing strains ended with the introduction of the concept of the aesthetic in the nineteenth century. While the second strain, the philosophy of art, has enjoyed a renewed interest in the twentieth century, the concept of the aesthetic has perhaps claimed even more attention from philosophers. Out of the tradition of Schopenhauer and others has developed a collection of theories which were called "aesthetic-attitude theories" in the sketch of aesthetics today at the end of Part I. As was also indicated in that sketch, the attitude theories have been challenged by the view called "metacriticism." The dispute between these two types of theory ultimately revolves around the issue of which view gives the correct account of the nature of the object of criticism and appreciation—the aesthetic object.

Chapter 5 of Part II is devoted to a discussion of three versions of the attitude theory. The first of the attitude views is the *psychical-distance theory* of Edward Bullough, which was published early in the present century.[1] Bullough's article is reprinted in most anthologies of aesthetics, and it has had enormous influence; it has become almost an article of faith for much present-day aesthetic theory. The second attitude view is the *theory of disinterested attention,* which is a descendent of Bullough's theory and has many adherents. I shall discuss this view as it is currently defended by Jerome Stolnitz[2] and Eliseo Vivas.[3] The third attitude theory is Virgil Aldrich's recently developed account[4] which makes the notion of *seeing as* the central notion.[5]

Chapter 6 of Part II is devoted to a discussion and criticism of Monroe Beardsley's metracritical version of aesthetic object.[6] In connection with this discussion I shall make some positive suggestions of my own toward a way of conceiving objects of criticism.

---

## Chapter 5. The Aesthetic Attitude

---

IT IS NOT completely clear what "attitude" means in the expression "aesthetic attitude," except that the acts and psychological states (attitudes?) of persons are essentially involved in the theories. Each of the three versions discussed here claims that a person can *do* something (achieve distance, perceive disinterestedly, or see as) which changes any object perceived into an aesthetic object. The reader can easily note the influence on the attitude theorists of Shaftesbury, Burke, Schopenhauer, and other earlier philosophers.

### The Aesthetic State: Psychical Distance

Edward Bullough introduces the concept of psychical distance by using as an example the appreciation of a natural phenomenon rather than a work of art. Consider, he says, how enjoyable various aspects of a fog at sea can be, even though to be in such a situation is dangerous. Bullough writes,

> Distance is produced in the first instance by putting the phenomenon, so to speak, out of gear with our practical, actual self; by allowing it to stand outside the context of our personal needs and ends—in short, by looking at it "objectively," as it has often been called, by permitting only such reactions on our part as emphasize the "objective" features of the experience. . . .[7]

Distance has an inhibitory aspect, a "putting [of the phenomenon] out of gear with our practical, actual self." The inhibition may be either an action of the perceiver or a psychological state into which the perceiver is induced; once it has occurred, an object can be aesthetically appreciated. "Distance" for Bullough is the name of a psychological state which can be achieved and which can be lost. He describes two ways in which distance can be lost, calling them cases of "over-distancing" and "under-distancing." His example of under-distancing is the case of a jealous husband at a performance of *Othello* who keeps thinking of his own wife's suspicious behavior. Sheila Dawson, a present-day follower of Bullough, gives as an example of over-distancing the case in which a person is primarily interested in the technical details of a performance.

It is perhaps significant that Bullough uses the appreciation of a natural entity which threatens the safety of the observer (a fog at sea) to introduce his theory of psychical distance. It seems natural to assume that there must be some psychological phenomenon which in some way removes the threat of harm to an observer so that he may appreciate the qualities of a threatening entity like a fog at sea. Bullough's account here is reminiscent of Schopenhauer's theory of the sublime. Schopenhauer speaks of the forcible detachment of the will (roughly the self) required for the appreciation of a sublime and threatening object. But do we need to postulate a special kind of action called "to distance" and a special kind of psychological state called "being distanced" in order to account for the fact that we can sometimes appreciate the characteristics of threatening things? Wouldn't it be simpler and more economical to explain this phenomenon in terms of *attention,* that is, as a case of focusing attention of some of the characteristics of, say, a fog at sea and ignoring others? In fact, one may be fully and painfully aware of the danger of the situation and still appreciate some of the characteristics of something like a fog at sea. Of course, there is no virtue in being theoretically economical if one ignores actual fact. The issue presumably has to be settled introspectively. Do we, in order to appreciate some object, commit a special act of distancing? Or, if in a given case it is not a question of doing something, are we ever induced into a state of being distanced when faced with a work of art or a natural object? It does not seem that either of these two kinds of things occurs.

Although the theory of psychical distance seems to have some initial plausibility when invoked to deal with threatening natural objects, it has very little when it is used to explain our relation to works of art. The jealous husband at *Othello* is not someone who has lost or failed to achieve something (psychical distance), he is simply someone who, for reasons peculiar to him, is having difficulty attending to the action of the play. A hypothetical case frequently used to illustrate the theory is that of a spectator who mounts the stage to save the threatened heroine. It is claimed that such a man would have lost psychical distance, but a better explanation would be that he has lost his mind and is no longer mindful of the rules and conventions which govern theater situations, in this case the rule which forbids spectators from interfering with the action of the play. There are similar conventions and rules for each established art form. Of course, in the case of some present-day theater productions, the participation of the audience is invited. One of the nonhypothetical examples used by some defenders of psychical distance to illustrate how the psychological state works actually throws suspicion on the theory. Both Sheila Dawson,[8] an explicit follower of Bullough, and Susanne Langer,[9] whose view that art is illusion is in some ways similar to Bullough's theory, make use of the scene in *Peter Pan* in which Peter Pan turns to the audience and asks them to clap their hands in order to save Tinkerbelle's life. It is claimed that Peter Pan's action destroys psychical distance (or the necessary illusion) and is a moment "when most children would like to slink out of the theater and not a few cry— not because Tinkerbelle may die, but because the magic is gone."[10] The claim is, in effect, that a theatrical device destroys or gravely impairs the status of *Peter Pan* as an aesthetic object, that is, as an object of aesthetic appreciation and experience. But before any theoretical conclusions are drawn from this alleged fact it should be determined if children actually are made "acutely miserable"[11] by Peter Pan's action and want to slink out of the theater. In fact, children respond enthusiastically to the appeal to participate in the play. Langer remembers that as a child the appeal caused her acute misery, but she also reports that all the other children clapped and enjoyed themselves! If we are to take account of actual responses in drawing theoretical conclusions, it seems most plausible to develop the theory along the lines of the response of the overwhelming majority. In addition, a little reflection reveals that many highly rated plays and movies employ devices similar to the one in *Peter Pan*— for example, *Our Town, A Taste of Honey,* and *Tom Jones.*

If the theory of psychical distance were simply a complicated and somewhat misleading way of talking about attending or not attending to things, there would be little reason to be concerned about it. Its defenders, however, see it as the first and key step of an aesthetic theory, and it is held to have far-reaching implications. The *Peter Pan* case shows that it is thought that the theory can provide a basis for evaluating works of art. It is also thought that being in a state of psychical distance can reveal the properties of a work of art which properly belong to the aesthetic object, that is, those properties to which we ought to direct our attention and from which our aesthetic experience ought to derive. In short, it is thought that substantive guidelines for art criticism and appreciation can be derived from the nature of a certain kind of psychological state. If there is no such psychological state, this approach is in serious difficulty.


## Aesthetic Awareness: Disinterested Attention

The view that the concept of the aesthetic can be defined in terms of disinterested perception, or attention, is an outgrowth of both the theory of psychical distance and the notion of disinterestedness in the eighteenth-century theories of taste. But whereas "psychical distance" is supposed to name a special action or psychological state, "disinterested attention" is held to name the ordinary action of attending done in a special way. The persuasiveness of this version of the aesthetic attitude depends entirely on the clarity and validity of the descriptions of the alleged disinterested attention to art and nature.

Jerome Stolnitz's definition of aesthetic attitude may be taken as a standard one. He defines it as the "disinterested (with no ulterior purpose) and sympathetic attention to and contemplation of any object of awareness whatever, for its own sake alone."[12] Eliseo Vivas's conception of aesthetic attitude is similar to Stolnitz's. Vivas uses the term "intransitive" rather than "disinterested" to refer to the crucial mode of attention, but the two terms have essentially the same meaning.

Let us consider some cases which are used to illustrate the disinterested-attention theory of the aesthetic. Suppose that person $A$ is listening to some music in order to write an analysis of it for an examination. Since $A$ has an ulterior purpose, he is not attending to the music disinterestedly. $A$'s attention to the music must therefore be interested, as contrasted with disinterested. Suppose that a person $B$ is looking at a painting and a figure depicted in the painting suddenly reminds him of someone he knows. $B$ then proceeds to muse about his acquaintance or perhaps to tell stories about the acquaintance, all the while standing before the painting. *B* is now using the painting as a vehicle for his associations and would, thereby, supposedly be attending to the painting in an interested fashion.

The disinterested-interested distinction is applied by its adherents quite generally to all the arts, but perhaps one more example will suffice for present purposes. Eliseo Vivas cites a number of ways in which literature may be attended to transitively, or interestedly: when it is read as history, social criticism, diagnostic evidence of an author's neurosis, or a springboard for free associations uncontrolled by the literary work. Remember that these are supposed to be nonaesthetic ways of attending to literature, and hence the objects of such attention are not supposed to be aesthetic objects. According to this theory, a work of art or a natural object may or may not be an aesthetic object, depending on whether or not it is attended to disinterestedly. The same object may be an aesthetic object on one occasion and not on another occasion.

The theory of disinterested, or intransitive, attention entails that there are at least two distinguishable kinds of attention and that the concept of the aesthetic can be defined in terms of one of them. The adherents of the theory explain disinterested attention in a negative way, describing and giving cases of what it is *not,* that is, cases of interested attention. Presumably, if the nature of interested attention can be made clear, we will have at least some idea of what disinterested attention is. The crucial question is, then, are the kinds of cases cited as instances of interested attention to works of art genuine cases of a species of attention? Perhaps there is only one kind of attention.

Consider the case of *B,* who fell to musing or telling stories while looking at a painting. Now although *B* is standing in front of the painting with his eyes turned toward it, he is not attending to the painting at all. He is attending to the objects of his musing or to the story he is telling. So this case of alleged nondisinterested attention to the painting turns out to be a case of inattention to the painting, not a special kind of attention at all. In another case, *B* might, say, be telling a story and still have his attention on the painting. Even in this case, however, there is no reason to think that there is more than one kind of attention involved. Consider the case of *A*, who was listening to music in preparation for an examination. He would have motives for what he is doing which are different from those of someone listening to the music with no such ulterior motives, but would this mean that the two persons are *attending* in a different way? They could both enjoy or be bored by the music, no matter what their motives are. In either case, attention might lapse, reawaken, drift, and so on. So although it is easy enough to see what it means to have different motives, it is not so easy to see how having different motives affects the nature of attention. Different motives may direct attention to different objects, but the activity of attention itself remains the same.

Finally, consider Vivas's contentions about literature as aesthetic object. One startling clue that something is wrong with the disinterested-attention theory is Vivas's claim that his conception of the aesthetic posits "that *The Brothers Karamazov* can hardly be read as art . . ."[13] that is, can hardly be experienced as an aesthetic object. Since *The Brothers Karamazov* is a great novel, it must surely be a paradigm case of an aesthetic object, and any theory that denies this must be suspect. Why isn't it, according to Vivas, an aesthetic object? Perhaps because he thinks its complexity and size prevent intransitive attention but most probably because one can hardly avoid reading it to some extent as social criticism, which is one of the ways that he mentions literature is attended to nonaesthetically. But are the kinds of cases mentioned by Vivas actually cases of transitive, or interested, attention to literary works? Two of the alleged cases of attending interestedly to a literary work are really ways of *not attending* to the work. To use the work as a springboard for free associations uncontrolled by the literary work is simply a case of losing touch with the work and ceasing to attend to it. Similarly, to use the work to diagnose the author's neurosis is a way of being distracted from the work, rather than a special way of attending to it. In some cases, one might still be attending in the usual way to some aspects of the work and at the same time be attending to (thinking about) the author's neurosis. These would be cases of partial distraction. In other cases, the distraction might be complete, with the author's neurosis becoming the sole object of attention.

The two other cases of alleged interested attending—reading literature as history or as social criticism—are quite different and are not cases of distraction. Works of literature sometimes contain historical references and social criticism. Assume that reading a work as, say, history means being aware that a historical reference is made by the work and perhaps even that it is correct or incorrect. How does one's attention differ in this case from the attention given when one is unaware that an actual historical reference is made or when the work is wholly fictional? Assume that reading a work as history means reading it simply or solely as history. Even this way of reading does not mark out a special kind of attention; it means only that a single aspect of a work is being attended to and that the many other aspects of the work are being ignored or missed. The historical or socially critical content, if any, of a literary work is a part of the work (although only a part), and any attempt to say that it is somehow not a part of the aesthetic object when other aspects of the work are, seems strange. Why should, say, an aspect as important as social criticism be segregated out of the aesthetic object? The disinterested-attention theorist argues that such a segregation is effected simply by a perceptual distinction— a certain kind of attention can take as its objects only certain kinds of objects. There is, however, a serious doubt that such a species of attention exists.

The alleged cases of interested attention may be summarized as follows: *A*'s attention to the music turned out to be just like that of any other listener; *B*'s interested attention to the painting turned out to be a case of not attending; free-associating and diagnosing the author's neurosis turned out also to be cases of not attending; attending to historical or socially critical content turned out to be simply attending to one aspect of literature. Many other examples of allegedly interested attention could be discussed, but if the ones analyzed are typical, the theory of disinterested attention cannot be a correct account of the aesthetic attitude and cannot be used as a basis for the description of the concept of aesthetic object.


## Aesthetic Perception: "Seeing As"


Virgil Aldrich has recently developed an aesthetic theory out of one of the central notions of the philosophy of Ludwig Wittgenstein. Aldrich's view is an aesthetic-attitude theory because he claims it is something which a subject *does* or has happen to him that determines whether an object is an aesthetic object or not. Whereas the previously discussed theories make use of the notion of a special psychological state or a special kind of attention, Aldrich's view posits an *aesthetic mode of perception.*

Although he did not make use of them for aesthetic theory, Wittgenstein called attention to ambiguous figures. A line drawing which sometimes looks like steps seen from above and sometimes like steps seen from below is an example of an ambiguous figure. The one made famous by Wittgenstein is "the duck-rabbit": a drawing sometimes seen as a duck's head and at other times as a rabbit's head. Aldrich leads into his theory by way of a discussion of ambiguous figures, noting that three things can be distinguished in the case of such figures. These are 1) the design the lines make on paper, 2) the representation of, say, a duck, and 3) the other representation of, say, a rabbit. Nothing that Aldrich says about ambiguous figures and the notion of "seeing as", which is used in describing such figures, is controversial.

Aldrich develops his aesthetic theory as a parallel of the perceptual phenomenon of ambiguous figures. He asserts that earlier theorists were mistaken in thinking that there is only one mode of perception. He claims there are two: the aesthetic mode and the nonaesthetic mode. The nonaesthetic mode he calls "observation" and the aesthetic mode he calls "prehension." Observation parallels the seeing of one of the representations in an ambiguous figure, and prehension parallels the seeing of the other representation. The object of observation is what Aldrich calls a "physical object," and the object of prehension is called an "aesthetic object." The parallel of the design itself Aldrich calls a "material object." A material object is seen as a physical object when observed and as an aesthetic object when prehended. The following diagram will make clear Aldrich's use of the parallel:

> Duck ...... (observation) ......physical object
> Design .......................material object
> Rabbit...... (prehension) ......aesthetic object

Aldrich's theory provides a neat solution to the problem of aesthetic object and from this point of view is admirable. It also avoids any commitment to disinterested attention or psychical distance, which were seen to involve difficulties. Finally, it purports to be a development out of one of the most powerful and influential philosophical movements of the present day, the philosophy of Wittgenstein. Is there, however, any reason to think that Aldrich's theory is true? Does he present conclusive evidence for his contention that there really are two modes of perception?

Aldrich explicitly states that his remarks about ambiguous figures are not supposed to be evidence for his aesthetic theory: they simply served to suggest the theory to him. The lack of an evidential relation between the two, however, must be made clear. The fact that a single design can function as two or more representations gives no evidence for two modes of perception. For example, the seeing of the duck representation is exactly like the seeing of the rabbit representation so far as the seeing is concerned. Only one kind of perception is involved, although the perception has two objects (representations) . The notion of *seeing as* may be useful in providing an analysis of the concept of representation but that is clearly another matter. The phenomenon of ambiguous figures is supposed to be a kind of model for Aldrich's theory. However, it is not even a complete model, for there are not two kinds of perception involved in the seeing of ambiguous figures.

The only evidence which Aldrich gives for his theory in the book in which he sets forth his view is the following alleged example of aesthetic perception.

> Take for example a dark city and a pale western sky at dusk, meeting at the sky line. In the purely . . . aesthetic view of this, the light sky area just above the jagged sky line protrudes toward the point of view. The sky is closer to the viewer than are the dark areas of buildings. This is the disposition of these material things in aesthetic space. . . .[14]

Almost everyone would agree that the experience described in this passage is an aesthetic experience and that it has aesthetic value. Doubtless, also, the sky could appear to be closer to the viewer than the actually closer buildings. The fact, however, that things look different and that visual relations appear to alter under varying conditions of lighting is no reason for thinking that there are two modes of perceiving which a person can switch off or on. At the end of the city-at-dusk example, Aldrich gives a general characterization of aesthetic perception which suggests that something is radically wrong with his whole approach. He writes that aesthetic perception "is, if you like, an 'impressionistic' way of looking, but still a mode of perception. . . ."[15] Independently of whether or not it makes sense to speak of an impressionistic way of looking, it is surely not the case that all the experiences we call aesthetic are impressionistic, although perhaps some are. What is impressionistic about watching *Hamlet,* looking at a Ming vase, or looking at a painting by Rembrandt? What, for that matter, is impressionistic about *looking* at an impressionistic painting or listening to impressionistic music?

Several years after the publication of his book, Aldrich offered another example to exemplify aesthetic perception and thereby serve as evidence for his theory.[16] He recalls watching illuminated snowflakes falling at night. If he focused his eyes at a point in the dark behind the snowflakes, the snowflakes appeared comet-shaped, tails up. Aldrich calls this an "impressionistic" way of looking at the snowflakes and contrasts it with the ordinary way of looking at them. The snowflakes case is different from the city-at-sunset case in that the observer actually does something—the trick of focusing his eyes. Nevertheless, the snowflake case does not serve as evidence for the theory that there are two ways of perceiving. While it is no doubt true that snowflakes perceived when one's eyes are focused behind them are aesthetically pleasing, it is also true that snowflakes are aesthetically pleasing when looked at in the ordinary way. There are many tricks that one can do which will produce new and unusual perceptual qualities. One may squint at snowflakes (or at a painting), look at them with a telescope or a microscope, look at them while under the influence of drugs, and so on. None of these tricks will serve to pick out just those perceptual qualities which are called "aesthetically pleasing." We may find some of these tricks useful on some occasions—as when we squint at a painting to screen out details in order to see its composition or structure. We do not, however, always or even frequently use such tricks when we look at paintings, watch plays, and so on. The "impressionistic" way of looking at snowflakes is no more a uniquely aesthetic way of looking than is the "impressionistic" way of looking at the city at sunset. One must conclude that Aldrich has given us no reasonable evidence for the truth of his theory.

## Summary and Conclusions

Aesthetic-attitude theories of the present day grew out of such nineteenth-century theories as that of Schopenhauer with its insistence on the aesthetic as a will-less, nonpractical state of contemplation. These theories have roots even further back in the eighteenth-century notion of disinterestedness. The attitude theories share with the eighteenth-century taste theories the view that a psychological analysis is the key to a correct theory. But they reject the eighteenth-century assumption that some particular feature of the world such as uniformity in variety triggers the aesthetic, or taste, response. The attitude theories share with the nineteenth-century aesthetic theories the view that any object (with certain reservations about the obscene and the disgusting) can become an object of aesthetic appreciation. But they reject the nineteenth-century assumption that aesthetic theory must be embedded in a comprehensive metaphysical system, e.g., Schopenhauer's philosophical system.

Theories of aesthetic attitude have three main goals. First and most basic, they attempt to isolate and describe the psychological factors which constitute the aesthetic attitude. Second, they attempt to develop a conception of aesthetic object as that which is the object of the aesthetic attitude. Third, they attempt to account for aesthetic experience by conceiving of it as the experience derived from an aesthetic object. For these theories, an aesthetic object has the function of being the proper locus of appreciation and criticism (criticism understood as including description, interpretation, and evaluation). The concept of aesthetic object has a normative function. That is, it is supposed somehow to guide our attention to the qualities of art and nature which are "aesthetically relevant" and thereby serve as a foundation for criticism. Recall how it was thought that the concept of psychical distance had evaluative implications for *Peter Pan* and that the concept of disinterested perception had evaluative implications for *The Brothers Karamazov*. Attitude theories held that these works of art contain elements which are not only aesthetically irrelevant but positively destructive to aesthetic values. It seems that each of these three influential versions of aesthetic attitude involves some fundamental difficulty. If this is so, then it seems reasonable to conclude that the attitude concept of aesthetic object with its attendant theory of criticism and aesthetic experience is also probably in difficulty. Is there a viable alternative which will provide a concept of aesthetic object and a basis for a theory of criticism? Metacriticism is thought by many to be such an alternative.

## Chapter 6. Metacriticism

To REPEAT WHAT WAS SAID in Part I, metacriticism is the philosophical activity which takes as its task the analysis and
clarification of the basic concepts that art critics use when
they describe, interpret, or evaluate particular works of art.
See the diagram at the end of Part I, and note that what is
called "aesthetic object" in Chapters 5 and 6 is labeled "object of criticism" in the diagram. Monroe Beardsley's theory
of aesthetic object will be discussed and criticized in this
chapter. This is not to suggest that Beardsley's view is the
only possible metacritical theory of aesthetic object. Beardsley's version is, however, the only one which is fairly
completely worked out. The summary of Beardsley's theory
presented here differs in two respects from his original
presentation. First, he does not formulate in any explicit way
the *principles* which are implicit in his argument, as is done
here. Second, the theory as formulated here concerns only
works of art and does not discuss natural objects. Neither of
these two differences violates the spirit or intent of his theory.

Beardsley shares with the attitude theorists the assumption
that there is a clear-cut way to distinguish aesthetic objects
from all other things, but he rejects the notion that it can be
done on the basis of aesthetic attitude. Although he does not
formulate explicit principles in developing his theory of
aesthetic object, Beardsley implicitly uses two: the principle
of distinctness and the principle of perceptibility. Although
he no doubt has it in mind throughout, the principle of distinctness is most clearly used in connection with Beardsley's
argument that the intention (what someone has in mind to
do) of the artist is not part of the aesthetic object. His argument very briefly is that although an artist's intention is

causally related to the work of art he produces, an intention is *distinct from* (not part of) an actual work. It follows that if something is not part of a work of art, it cannot be part of an aesthetic object. Beardsley has many other things to say about this topic, but this is the core of his argument.

The *principle of distinctness* may be formulated in the following way: in order for something to be part of an aesthetic object, it must be part of, not distinct from, a work of art. (An analysis of the concept "work of art" will not be given until Part III of this book, but the expression "work of art" is being used here in the classificatory, nonevaluative sense; however, it is not being used as a synonym for "aesthetic object.") Please remember that the current discussion of aesthetic objects is limited to the domain of art. Natural objects may, of course, be aesthetic objects, but they are not under discussion here. A brief remark about natural objects as aesthetic objects is made at the end of this chapter. Assuming that the principle of distinctness is acceptable and that its application in the case concerning intention is correct, something more is obviously needed to sort out the widely differing aspects of works of art.

It is clear that it would be silly to take many of the aspects of works of art as parts of the aesthetic object. For example, the color of the back of a painting or the actions of the stage-hands backstage at the performance of a play are surely not properly objects of appreciation and criticism. The situation as it stands at this point may be represented by the following table, in which two aspects of a painting are used by way of illustration.

| Works of Art | All Other Objects |
|---|---|
| a. The arrangement of the colors on the front surface of a painting | |
| b. The color of the back of a painting | |

The principle of distinctness has drawn the vertical line which separates works of art from all else, but a horizontal line is now needed to separate those aspects of a work of art which properly belong to an aesthetic object from those that do not.

Drawing upon a long tradition which emphasizes the importance of sensory elements in aesthetics, Beardsley attempts to use the distinction between the nonperceptible (which he calls the "physical") and the perceptible. This *principle of perceptibility* may be formulated in the following way: in order for something to be part of an aesthetic object, it must be perceptible under the normal conditions of experiencing the kind of art in question. The qualification about normal conditions must be added because, for example, the color of the back of a painting is perceptible, but not under the normal conditions of viewing paintings. This second principle draws the horizontal line and completes the diagram.

|  | Works of Art | All Other Objects |
|---|---|---|
| Perceptible | a. The arrangement of the colors on the front surface of a painting | |
| Imperceptible | b. The color of the back of a painting | |

The two principles may be formulated as one and called "principle *N*":

In order for something to be part of an aesthetic object it must be part of a work of art and be perceptible under normal conditions.

Principle *N* states that the two conditions are *necessary conditions* for something to be an aesthetic object. If principle *N* were the only principle concerning aesthetic object which Beardsley uses, then something could be part of a work of art and be perceptible under normal conditions but not be part of an aesthetic object. It is, however, possible that Beardsley's theory assumes not only that each of the two conditions is individually necessary but also that they are *jointly sufficient* for something to be part of an aesthetic object. Thus, Beardsley may hold to what may be called "principle *S*":

> If something is part of a work of art and is perceptible under normal conditions, then it is part of an aesthetic object.

However, Beardsley's theory of aesthetic object is in difficulty regardless of whether it contains only principle *N* or contains both *N* and *S*. Let us call the version of the theory which contains both *N* and *S* the strong version and the version which contains only *N* the weak version. (In private correspondence, Beardsley denies that he holds the strong version unless the "normal conditions" are spelled out in such a way as to rule out the kind of counterinstances which I produce in my argument against the strong version.)

The difficulties can best be revealed by considering four cases, the first and third of which involve aspects of works of art which are perceptible and the second and fourth of which involve aspects of works of art which are not perceptible under normal conditions. The first two cases raise no problem for the theory, but the last two are counterinstances to Beardsley's theory. All the cases are from the theater, which provides a rich complexity of elements.

First, consider the case of the onstage performance of an actor in *Hamlet*. Clearly the performance is recognizable as part of an aesthetic object, i.e., part of that which is properly appreciated and criticized. The performance is both part of a work of art and is perceptible under normal conditions. It is therefore consistent with principle *N* (the weak version) that the performance is part of an aesthetic object and it deductively follows from principle *S* (the strong version) that the performance is part of an aesthetic object. This case raises no problems for Beardsley.

Second, consider the case of the stagehands in traditional theater productions. Although the work of the stagehand is necessary for a performance of the actors, the performance of the stagehands is clearly not part of an aesthetic object. The performance of the stagehands is part of a work of art in a broad sense but it is not perceptible to the audience under normal conditions. It deductively follows from principle $N$ that the performance of the stagehands is not part of an aesthetic object. This second case does not raise any problems for Beardsley.

Third, consider the case of the property man in traditional Chinese theater, who appears on stage while the action of the play is in progress and moves props around, shifts scenery, and so on. A similar case closer to home is that of the stagehands of theater in the round, who move scenery and props in full view of the audience, although they usually do so between acts. It is doubtful that either the Chinese property man or theater-in-the-round stagehands would be considered part of an aesthetic object. Nevertheless, it deductively follows from principle $S$ that both are part of an aesthetic object, since both are part of a work of art and are perceptible under normal conditions. Perhaps it can be argued that the theater-in-the-round stagehands are not seen under normal conditions, since they are seen between acts, and hence that it does not follow from principle $S$ that they are part of the aesthetic object. This argument cannot, however, be used in the case of the Chinese property man, for he is seen under normal conditions. The strong version is thus shown to be inadequate because it entails the false conclusion that a Chinese property man is part of an aesthetic object.

Fourth, consider the hypothetical case of a ballet dancer who uses imperceptible wires in order to make incredible leaps. The imperceptible wires are part of the aesthetic object because it would be necessary to know if such wires were being used in order to appreciate and criticize the performance correctly. A given leap might be magnificent if wires were not being used but mediocre if wires were being used. The wires would be an integral part of the performance.[17]

However, it deductively follows from principle $N$ that the wires are not part of an aesthetic object, since although they are part of a work of art, they are imperceptible under normal conditions. The weak version is thus shown to be inadequate because it entails the false conclusion that the imperceptible wires are not part of an aesthetic object.

To summarize, the case of the Chinese property man (and any similar case) shows the strong version to be inadequate and the hypothetical case of the ballet dancer on imperceptible wires (and any similar case) shows the weak version to be inadequate. Since the Chinese property man is perceptible and not part of an aesthetic object and the wires are imperceptible and are, it is clear that the principle of perceptibility is the major defect in Beardsley's theory.

## Concluding Remarks

Unlike the attitude theorists who seem to be wrong in a very basic way, Beardsley's difficulty seems more a matter of detail. Perhaps, then, an adequate metacritical theory of aesthetic object may be worked out by following the trail which Beardsley has blazed.[18]

Perhaps the principle of distinctness can be applied a second time to yield the desired results. In its first use, this principle was used to distinguish art from nonart. Perhaps the principle can be applied *within* the category of art to distinguish those aspects of a work of art which belong to an aesthetic object from those which do not. This second application would come off if, upon inspection and reflection, the various aspects of works of art fall into two distinct classes, one containing all and only those aspects which it is proper to appreciate and criticize. These aspects would constitute aesthetic objects.

However, by this time it may already be evident that the principle of distinctness in its first use cannot actually be applied in a simple, straightforward way. Knowing whether something is distinct from a work of art presupposes that one already knows what kinds of things are and are not parts of works of art. Determining whether or not something is part of a work of art is actually a case of *realizing*, on the basis of what one knows about works of the type in question, that a given thing is or is not a part. There will no doubt be cases of artistic innovation concerning which very little information is available and for which conventions have not been established—perhaps this is the case for "happenings." Time will take care of these cases in one way or another. Even if the determination of distinctness between things which are and are not parts of a work of art cannot be made in an easy way, it does seem that it can be made. And if this is so, it encourages one to think that a second and similar kind of determination of distinctions can be made *within* the category of art. That is, on the basis of what one knows about the various types of art and the conventions and rules which govern their presentation, one can come to realize which aspects are the proper aspects for appreciation and criticism. The realization at either of the two levels will not always or even typically be easy. In many cases, a great deal of thought will be necessary and controversy will certainly not be easily settled. The controversy, for example, over whether or not the intention of the artist is part of a work of art is still hotly debated. It is worth noting that the abandoned principle of perceptibility cannot be applied in a simple, straightforward way either; perceptibility is qualified by "under the normal conditions of experiencing the kind of art in question," which indicates that perceptibility is not established independently of the concept of a particular type of art.

To sum up, it seems that a conception of aesthetic object can be arrived at but not in the clean-cut way that either the attitude theorists or Beardsley had hoped. What it makes sense to appreciate and criticize in the case of a given work of art cannot be known *antecedent to* a rich experience of and full understanding of works of art of the type in question. Thus the method of arriving at a concept of aesthetic object will have to be piecemeal reflection on one type of art at a time. The concept produced by this procedure will be complicated and variegated, but this simply reflects the complexity of the arts.

There are two matters which it seems appropriate to mention at this point. First, Beardsley's view of aesthetic object as it is formulated here and that of the attitude theorists are different in scope. According to the latter, anything —work of art or natural thing—may become an aesthetic object, whereas Beardsley's view does not include an account of natural objects as aesthetic objects. This is not surprising because metacriticism takes as its subject matter criticism which takes as its subject matter art, not natural objects. In order for metacriticism to be a complete aesthetic theory, some account which deals with natural objects must be added to it. There is not space to pursue this topic here, but perhaps the account might be developed along these lines: a natural object is an aesthetic object when it functions in someone's experience in a manner similar to the way a work of art functions when it is taken as an object of appreciation and/or criticism.

Second, it may seem appropriate at this point to have a discussion of the nature of aesthetic experience. However, insofar as the attitude theorists are concerned, aesthetic experience seems to mean "that experience which is had when in the aesthetic attitude." Thus, for the attitude theories, the concept of aesthetic experience has, in effect, already been discussed. Beardsley, however, has an explicit theory of aesthetic experience, arguing that it has certain specific characteristics which differentiate it from ordinary experience. Since Beardsley's theory of aesthetic experience is so closely related to his account of evaluation, it seems best to leave a discussion of it until Part V.

# PART III

---

# Present-Day Theories
# of Art

---

PART I contained outlines of two theories, or philosophies, of art: the imitation theory, which dates from ancient times, and the expression theory, which came into prominence in the nineteenth century. Five recent theories of art will be discussed in this chapter. Of these five, two—Susanne Langer's and R. G. Collingwood's—are descendents of the two earlier philosophies, one—Clive Bell's—is closely related to the traditional theory of beauty, and two—Morris Weitz's and my own—are of more recent origin. Each of the first four of these theories has played a prominent part in the development of twentieth-century aesthetics, and the theories are representative of the major trends in the philosophy of art of today and the recent past. Bell's theory of significant form, which is discussed first, may be thought of as a theory that developed out of the Platonic theory of beauty. Although it now has few, if any, adherents, the concept of significant form was very influential in the early years of this century. Langer's theory of expressive symbolism may be thought of as a modern version of the imitation theory, although she probably would not wish it to be understood that way. At the present time, her conception of the arts as symbolic forms is probably the most popular theory of art as far as the general public is concerned. However, her views have been severely criticized by many philosophers. Collingwood's theory of imaginative expression is a sophisticated version of the expression theory, which continues to be a powerful tradition with a number of adherents. Weitz's analysis of the concept of art is an attempt to adapt some of the insights of the philosophy of Ludwig Wittgenstein to the theory of art. Weitz's conception of art as an open concept probably has more adherents today among philosophers than any other single view. The institutional theory of art which is developed in reaction to Weitz's views is my own attempt to sketch out a basis for a philosophy of art.

---

## Chapter 7.  A Modern Beauty Theory of Art

---

CLIVE BELL's book, entitled simply *Art,*[1] has achieved the status of a modern classic, the simplicity and lucidity of its argument having gained it a wide audience and great influence. The book incorporates many of the recurrent elements of aesthetic theory, and it is the origin of the expression "significant form," which for a time achieved wide currency and is still invoked by some today. Bell's theory is, then, a good one with which to begin a discussion of the philosophy of art. However, it should be borne in mind that Bell qualifies his remarks by stating that he is talking only about *visual* art, although at one point he suggests that his theory might also hold for music.

Bell's theory in many respects, especially in a basic underlying assumption, resembles that of Plato, but the most immediate influence on Bell was the English philosopher G. E. Moore, who was himself something of a Platonist. Moore, in working out his *ethical* theory, developed what has been called "the open-question argument," which has had great influence in ethics.[2] Bell attempted to adapt the conclusion of Moore's argument to aesthetics. Moore examined several traditional definitions of "good," arguing in each case that the open-question argument proved the definitions defective. Consider, for example, the hedonistic definition that "good" means "pleasure." Moore agrees that many pleasures are good but denies that "good" is *identical in meaning* with "pleasure" because he claims one can significantly ask of some given pleasure, "Is this pleasure good?" Moore's point is that if "good" and "pleasure" had the same meaning, it would be as silly to ask such a question as to ask, "Is this bachelor married?" When we carefully consider the question of whether a given pleasure is good, it will become clear to us, Moore contends, that it is not a silly question. It is simply an *open question* whether some pleasure is good or not. It can be seen from this example that Moore is concerned with the *meanings* of ethical terms, or concepts, and that he is assuming that the criterion of the correctness of definition of such moral concepts is our intuitive understanding of them.

Moore actually applied his analysis to only a few definitions of "good," but he thought that it undermined *all* such definitions, and he concludes that "good" cannot be defined. In addition, Moore concludes that "good" designates a simple, unanalyzable, nonnatural quality which characterizes some actions and states of affairs. The alleged fact that good is simple and unanalyzable means that it cannot be broken down into parts and hence cannot be defined. For example, the Greek concept of "man" can be broken down into *rationality* and *animality,* yielding the definition, "Man" means "rational animal." When Moore says that good is a nonnatural quality, he means that it is not an empirical quality perceived by the senses, like a color or a tone. The mind *intuits* rather than sees, hears, etc., that an action or state of affairs is good. Moore's notion of intuition is similar to Plato's concept of the knowing of nonempirical Forms. Also, like Plato, Moore makes an *essentialistic* assumption in developing his conception of goodness. He writes, ". . . we must discover what is both common and peculiar to all undoubted ethical judgments."[3] His view is essentialistic because he assumes that a *single essence* characterizes the objects of all judgments of goodness, namely, the quality of goodness itself. (In Chapter 10, the attack of Morris Weitz on essentialism in the theory of art will be discussed.)

The basic components of Bell's theory are three: 1) the phenomenological starting point, 2) his methodological assumption, and 3) his main conclusion. The first component is something he calls "the aesthetic emotion" and the third is "significant form," which he claims every work of art has. The second component is the assumption of essentialism, which relates the other two components, allowing significant form to be derived from the aesthetic emotion. Two quotations from the first chapter of Bell's book reveal the structure of his argument.

> The starting-point of all systems of aesthetics must be the personal experience of a peculiar emotion. The objects that provoke this emotion we call works of art. All sensitive people agree that there is a peculiar emotion provoked by works of art. . . . This emotion is called the aesthetic emotion.[4]

> . . . if we can discover some quality common and peculiar to all the objects that provoke [the aesthetic emotion], we shall have solved what I take to be the central problem of aesthetics. We shall have discovered the essential quality of a work of art . . . For either all works of visual art have some common quality, or when we speak of "works of art" we gibber. . . . What is this quality? . . . Only one answer seems possible— significant form.[5]

Bell begins by turning inward and claims to be able to distinguish a peculiarly aesthetic emotion which is not to be confused with the ordinary emotions of life such as fear, joy, anger, and such. He then turns outward and claims to discover that the objects which stimulate the aesthetic emotion are works of art. Finally, he attempts to discover what is common and peculiar to works of art by virtue of which they stimulate the aesthetic emotion, and he claims that this characteristic is significant form.

Bell is frequently criticized for arguing in a circle, that is, of saying when asked what the aesthetic emotion is that it is the emotion provoked by significant form and of saying when asked what significant form is that it is the object which provokes the aesthetic emotion. Perhaps Bell's way of expressing himself does leave him open to this charge, but he clearly intends to claim that the aesthetic emotion can be distinguished and isolated from all other emotions and that it can serve as a foundation for his philosophy of art. The most telling criticism which could be brought against Bell would be to show that there is no aesthetic emotion. However, it is perhaps impossible to show this because of the way in which he states his claim. If Jones maintains that he cannot discover the aesthetic emotion in his experience, Bell can answer that Jones must be insensitive (or has not had sufficient experience), because "All sensitive people agree that there is a peculiar emotion . . . the aesthetic emotion." The problem is that if one cannot discover the aesthetic emotion in one's own experience, then there must be the nagging suspicion that one is perhaps not sensitive enough and that one's experience is therefore not really a counterinstance to Bell's theory. Sheer numbers will not help either; there may simply be large numbers of insensitive people. Perhaps the best one could do by way of a test would be to see if persons who enjoy, are knowledgeable about, and frequently experience art and who are philosophically sophisticated enough to understand the issue claim to have the aesthetic emotion. At the present time, such persons do not seem to make such a claim, and it therefore seems that there is good reason to think that Bell is wrong in believing there is a peculiarly aesthetic emotion. Still, such a test would be difficult to set up and interpret definitively, and perhaps we must remain in some doubt.

At this point, it might seem that Bell's essentialistic assumption should be discussed. However, essentialism will be discussed in detail in Chapter 10 and is omitted here.

Before getting into a discussion of significant form, it will be helpful to give a general characterization of the term "form." By the form of a work of art is meant the total set of relations which obtain among the elements. (Homogeneous areas of color, for example, are elements of a work of art.)

Consider a design which is made up of thirteen dots as elements.

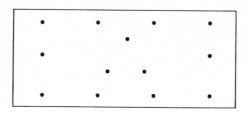

The form of the design is the total set of relations which obtain among the thirteen dots. Some of the relations assume more importance in the design than others: the ten dots around the edge of the design tend to form themselves into four straight lines forming a rectangle which encloses the three dots in the center, and these dots constitute themselves into three straight lines forming a triangle. Note that although all thirteen of the elements of the design are mentioned in the previous sentence, not all the relations were mentioned. For example, the straight-line relation between the upper left-hand dot and the dot at the apex of the triangle was not mentioned because it has no significance in this design. The relations which assume importance or the greatest importance in a design are called its "composition," or "structure," or even its "form." This last use of "form" is clearly not identical with the one under discussion, but the two notions are related.

Bell has maintained that all works of art must have some quality in common, but what is it?

> Only one answer seems possible—significant form. In each [of the works of art he has just mentioned], lines and colours combined in a particular way, certain forms and relations of forms, stir our aesthetic emotions. These relations and combinations of lines and colours, these aesthetically moving forms, I call "Significant Form"; and "Significant Form" is the one quality common to all works of visual art.[6]

On first reading, it appears that Bell is setting forth a view which may be called Hutchesonian because of its resemblance to the view of the eighteenth-century philosopher. Hutcheson maintained that uniformity in variety (significant form) triggered the sense of beauty (the aesthetic emotion). In this Hutchesonian reading, "significant form" becomes the name of a certain set of relations, which means that only two components are involved in the interpretation: a set of relations and the aesthetic emotion. However, because of the great influence of Moore on Bell and because of the nuances of the way in which he states his view, there is a possibility that Bell's theory should be given an intuitionist interpretation which is a bit more complicated than the Hutchesonian. In the passage quoted above, Bell says that "significant form" is the name of certain sets of relations, but he also says that significant form is a *quality*. Philosophers have traditionally used the terms "relation" and "quality" to refer to distinct and contrasting things. There seem, then, to be two possible versions of Bell's theory: the Hutchesonian one, which holds that "significant form" is the name of certain sets of relations, and the intuitionist version, which holds that "significant form" is the name of a nonnatural *quality* which certain sets of relations have. The intuitionist version involves three components: 1) the aesthetic emotion, 2) certain sets of relations, 3) and the nonnatural quality which certain sets of relations have and which is named by the expression "significant form." Which of these two versions did Bell hold? The drift of most of his remarks seems to support the Hutchesonian interpretation. Nevertheless, he also continues to speak of significant form as a quality. Late in his book, when he is discussing changes that art has undergone throughout history, he says, "So, though the essential quality—significance—is constant, in the choice of forms there is perpetual change."[7] Here "significance" is used alone, not coupled with "form," as the name of a quality, and this provides some evidence for the intuitionist version that significant form, or significance, is a nonnatural quality which *accompanies* certain forms on certain occasions. Perhaps, however, the best explanation of this situation is that Bell is not philosophically sophisticated enough to realize all the implications of his remarks and vocabulary, much of which was borrowed from one of the most acute analytic philosophers of the twentieth century, G. E. Moore.

Bell does not get around to providing a specific definition of "art" or "work of art," but he clearly indicates the following formulation: a work of art is an object which possesses significant form, significant form being the name of whatever stimulates the aesthetic emotion. A question which arises immediately is whether or not a natural object can have significant form and thereby be a work of art. Bell remarks that occasionally people "see in nature what we see in art,"[8] but he thinks this exceedingly rare. With this qualification in mind, perhaps it is accurate to say that for Bell a work of art is an *artifact* which possesses significant form.

But now a paradox seems to arise from the definition. It is clear from what Bell says throughout his book that not every object ordinarily called a "work of art" is a work of art by his definition. The paradox is that there seem to be works of art which are not works of art. However, the paradox is resolved when it is remembered that there are at least two senses of "work of art." There is the classificatory sense, in which all paintings, statues, vases, buildings, and such are works of art; but clearly Bell is not explicating this sense. There is also the evaluative sense, in which the expression "work of art" is used to praise artifacts and sometimes even natural objects. Bell's definition must be seen as an attempt to isolate the meaning of this second sense of "work of art," and this is the reason his theory is called a beauty theory of art in the title of this chapter. Beauty in either of its traditional meanings—as the name of some empirical characteristics or as the name of the Platonic Form of Beauty—carries with it an evaluative aspect. To say of something that it is beautiful is to praise it.

Is Bell's definition an adequate one? Since it is based upon the notion of the aesthetic emotion, the definition inherits all the obscurities involved in that slippery notion. Also, it seems plausible to demand that an adequate theory of art furnish explications of all the basic senses of "work of art," and Bell's theory does not deal at all with the classificatory sense. The two senses of "work of art" will be dealt with at some length in Chapters 10 and 11.

No discussion of Bell's view should omit at least mention of his famous conclusion concerning the value of representation in visual art. From what has been said thus far it should be clear that Bell thought that the formal relations within works of visual art are the source of great value, and surely he is correct in this matter. However, Bell drew a much stronger conclusion than this, namely, that representation in visual art has no aesthetic value at all and is often an aesthetic disvalue. He writes,

> Let no one imagine that representation is bad in itself; a realistic form may be as significant, in its place as part of the design, as an abstract. But if a representative form has value, it is as form, not as representation. The representative element in a work of art may or may not be harmful; always it is irrelevant.[9]

As Bell makes clear elsewhere, his claim is that representation is irrelevant to aesthetic value, although he readily admits that representation may have value of a nonaesthetic kind. His justification for distinguishing between two kinds of value is based upon the notion of the aesthetic emotion. He thinks that only formal relations can evoke the aesthetic emotion and that representation cannot. Representations may depict, suggest, and evoke the ordinary emotions of life such as fear, joy, and so on, but never the aesthetic emotion.

As vague and unconvincing as Bell's theoretical justification is for denying the significance of representation, his conclusion played an important role in art criticism and in the shaping of taste in the period after *Art* appeared. Bell's theory of art served as a basis for the critical attack on the sentimental, illustrative art which so dominated English taste of the time. Popular representative art largely neglected the formal aspects of painting, and Bell and others sought to change people's minds about such art. Bell was one of those who was responsible for introducing the English public to the paintings of Cézanne and other French Post-Impressionist painters of the time. A dubious theory of art was, then, responsible in part for an important development in the history of art and taste.

---

## Chapter 8.  A Modern Imitation Theory of Art

---

SUSANNE LANGER, who also emphasizes form in art, has set forth in a series of books, *Philosophy in a New Key*,[10] *Feeling and Form*,[11] and *Problems of Art*,[12] a philosophy of art which is one of the most influential of the present day. Unfortunately, her views are illustrative of many of the intellectual difficulties which are rife in aesthetics: pretentious language, misleading terminology, vagueness, and unnecessary mystery and complication. Although she presents her theory as the view that art is an *expressive symbolism,* it is misleading to so describe it, and close inspection reveals that it is a version of the imitation theory adapted to accommodate emotion and feeling.

Briefly put, Langer's theory of art consists of 1) a definition of art and 2) a thesis about how art functions. The theory rests on seven basic and variously interrelated technical notions: symbol, abstraction, expressiveness, feeling, form, illusion, and virtual image. The first five of these are involved in the definition and the last two (they are really one) in the thesis about art's function.

Langer is convinced that "art is essentially one," which means that she thinks a definition of art in terms of necessary and sufficient conditions can be given. The definition she gives is, "Art is the creation of forms symbolic of human feeling."[13] The two of the five technical notions which do not explicitly appear in this definition are abstraction and expressiveness, but they are implicit in her notion of symbol.

A symbol is expressive of human feeling by means of abstraction. What this seems to mean is that a work of art is by definition an *iconic* symbol of human feeling, although Langer does not explicitly use the words "iconic" or "iconic symbol." An iconic symbol is a symbol which resembles in some way what it signifies; for example, a highway sign with two crossed lines is an iconic symbol because the sign resembles the crossroads it signifies. Most symbols are not iconic. It should be made clear at the outset that Langer explicitly distinguishes art as symbol—what she calls the "art symbol"—from symbols in art.[14] Symbols in art are elements in works of art, such as depictions of halos, lambs, and so on, which symbolize qualities such as holiness and love. An art symbol is the work of art as a whole, and an art symbol may or may not contain symbols of the symbol-in-art type.

Each of the arts symbolizes in its own way "human feeling." "Music is a tonal analogue of emotive life."[15] "As *scene* is the basic abstraction of pictorial art, and *kinetic volume* of sculpture, that of architecture is an *ethnic* domain."[16] Similar statements are made about the other species of art. Presumably it is meant that music symbolizes emotional feelings, pictorial art symbolizes scenes of various kinds, and so on. It is at this point that the theory is vague. For example, in what sense does *scene* necessarily involve human feeling? Langer's definition raises two basic questions: 1) is art a symbol? and 2) is the subject matter of art always human feeling?

What does she mean by "symbol"? "A symbol is any device whereby we are enabled to make an abstraction."[17] But what, then, does "abstraction" mean? A form is abstract when it is *abstracted* or "removed" from its usual context.[18] Thus a form becomes a symbol when it is abstracted from its usual context; at least, this seems to be what is meant in the case of the *art* symbol. Thus, for example, a drawing of a woman would be an abstraction because the form of the drawing is less than the form of the whole context in which the woman who was the model exists. This drawing would be, in Langer's sense, a symbol, and since every work of art is like the drawing in this sense, every work of art is, therefore, an art symbol. Incidentally, this example should not be taken as indicating that every work of art must have some actual thing as a model.

Even though representation (depiction of objects in space) seems to satisfy Langer's definition of symbol, it turns out that she is not interested in representation. As she states, buildings, pots, and tunes are not representational, and her theory demands that all works of art have some single feature in common.

> Representational works, if they are good art, are so for the same reason as non-representational ones. They have more than one symbolic function—representation . . . and also artistic expression, which is presentation of ideas of feeling.[19]

All works of art are also, then, art symbols in this second sense. All works abstract and thereby symbolize human feeling, but feeling is not symbolized by means of representation. It is extremely difficult to understand Langer on this point, but presumably all works resemble the forms of human feeling but not to such a degree that the resemblance would constitute representation. A work of art symbolizes in this sense of "artistic expression" when

> It formulates the appearance of feeling, of subjective experience, the character of so-called "inner life," which . . . the normal use of words . . . is peculiarly unable to articulate, and which therefore we can only refer to in a general and quite superficial way.[20]

Langer's use of the term "symbol" has been strongly criticized by a number of philosophers.[21] The nub of the criticism is that by definition a symbol is something which signifies something else by virtue of either an explicit or a tacit convention, and that Langer's notion of art symbol does not have the required conventional aspect. Remember that an art symbol is the work as a whole and that every work is a unique art symbol. Thus there is the paradox of a unique, one-shot symbol. Contrast an art symbol with a symbol in art, say, a halo. The halo is a highly conventionalized entity and has appeared repeatedly throughout a long tradition. The characteristic of Langer's art symbol which is supposed to enable its symbolic function is its iconicity of human feelings. However, iconicity without convention is not enough to make something a symbol; if it were, almost everything would be a symbol of something, since almost everything is to some degree iconic of something else. For example, one table resembles another table, but we would not therefore conclude that either table is a symbol of the other. Even iconic symbols are established by convention, the crossroads highway sign, for example. Thus it is difficult to see how a work of art as a whole can be symbolic, as it lacks the necessary conventional aspect.

Langer came to feel the weight of such criticisms and declared that a work of art is not a "genuine symbol" and said that henceforth she would use the expression "expressive form" rather than "art symbol." However, even in the essay in which she accepts the criticism, she continues to use "art symbol" interchangeably with "expressive form." And as a kind of parting shot she adds, "Yet the function of what I called 'the art symbol' . . . is more *like* a symbolic function than like anything else."[22] Why does she cling so to the notion of symbolism? Because not only is it the central idea of her philosophy of art, it is the only thing which makes her theory novel and significant. Semantic notions like "symbol" have assumed a very important place in recent philosophy, and it would be a significant philosophical contribution to show that these ideas have an application in aesthetics and the philosophy of art.

Without the glamorous notion of symbol, Langer's theory turns out to be simply a version of the imitation theory of art. Works of art in some not very clear way are iconic of or imitate human feelings. Note that it is an imitation theory with a limited subject matter. In Plato's theory, the representation of a woman in a painting would count as an imitation, but in Langer's view, only human feeling is the universal subject matter of art. Even what is generally thought of as the most original feature of this theory, namely, the contention that music is symbolic (imitative) of human feeling, was in part anticipated by Aristotle, who maintained that the music of the flute, lyre, and pipes is imitation.

But enough has been said about symbolism. We come to the second aspect of Langer's definition of art, the claim that all art has as its subject matter feeling or, as she puts it, that art "formulates the appearance of feeling." Is it true that all art does this? The great difficulty with evaluating the claim is its vagueness. There do seem to be some cases in which art is iconic of feeling. Beardsley suggests that Ravel's "Bolero" may be iconic of some psychological process or other,[23] and some music *is* expressive of longing, sadness, and so on. But is it true that all music is iconic? And of what human feeling is a Mondrian painting iconic? It is difficult to say more on this point and the reader may simply evaluate for himself the claim that art is the appearance of feeling.

Langer's thesis about how art functions is that art is an *illusion*. Or to use another of her technical terms, every work of art is a *virtual image*. Although it cannot be asserted with complete assurance, "illusion" and "virtual image" seem to have essentially the same meaning in her theory. In discussing the pictorial art, she explains one in terms of the other.

> This purely visual space is an illusion, for our sensory experiences do not agree on it in their report . . . Like the space "behind" the surface of a mirror, it is what the physicists call "virtual space"—an intangible image.[24]

"Our sensory experiences do not agree" means that there is an appearance of objects in space but that they cannot be touched or felt. Perhaps it can also be said that in all but a very few cases of pictorial art the appearance of objects in space is recognizably different from that of our ordinary experience. Calling a work of art an "illusion" or a "virtual image" makes the point that there is a sense in which it is somehow different from objects encountered in our ordinary experience: a painting and its space are not the same as a window and its view; a stage murder is not the same as an actual one; and so on. No one can take exception to this obviously true point.

However, if Langer's claim is not disputable, her term "illusion" is subject to criticism as misleading. It suggests that art fools or deceives people, and although on rare occasions people are deceived, this is not typical. She recognizes the problem and explicitly declares that she is not claiming that people are deluded by art. Still, it is perverse to use the term, since its ordinary meaning involves deception as its dictionary definition reveals: "1. An unreal or misleading image . . . 2. State or fact of being deceived . . . 3. A perception which fails to give the true character of an object perceived."[25] She has taken a term with an established meaning, altered its meaning and turned it into a technical term. It is not surprising that her readers have been confused. Other terms she uses in this connection—"semblance" and "virtual image"—better convey her meaning. To call the space in a painting a "virtual space" or a "semblance of space" conveys that it is not a real space but does not suggest that deception is involved.

How important is the claim that art creates an illusion? No one thinks that he can stick his hand through a painting as through a window or that a dancer's gesture exists in the same context as the usher's gesture. To insist on this point seems somewhat odd. This insistence is perhaps due to the tradition in aesthetics that spectators are always or at least sometimes in danger of confusing art with reality—stage murders with real ones, for example. As was remarked in Chapter 5, Langer's theory of illusion is similar to the theory of psychical distance. However, not only is talk about illusion not really informative, there is also some danger in it. For as the *Peter Pan* case showed us, to talk about art as illusion suggests that there is some illusion that may be shattered and therefore that certain limitations must be placed on the techniques of art.

Finally, Langer's view of art also illustrates another common difficulty—confusing the definition of art with a statement of what makes art good. This comes out clearly when she tries to justify calling art a symbol. She says that art may be called a symbol because it fulfills a certain function, namely, it formulates the appearance of feeling, and "this function every good work of art does perform."[26] This remark about good art is pointless, because if Langer's theory is correct, *all* art—good and bad—formulates the appearance of feeling. The main point at issue here is that the conception of art must be independent of the criterion of good art, otherwise we would be unable to speak of bad art and we do in fact frequently speak of bad art. Langer blurs this distinction.

---

## Chapter 9.  A Modern Expressionist Theory of Art

---

R. G. COLLINGWOOD in *The Principles of Art*[27] develops a comprehensive and influential expressionist theory of art. He attempts to work out systematically and on a large philosophical scale the widely held view that there is an essential connection between art and the expression of emotion. His book is a sustained and complex argument in support of his conclusion that *art is imaginative expression.*

The basis for Collingwood's theory of art is his analysis of the concept of *craft,* in which he argues that art and craft are completely distinct. What he calls "the technical theory of art," which begins with Plato and persists to the present day, maintains that art and craft are species of a single genus. Collingwood denies that art and craft share a common essential feature and combats the technical theory of art in whatever form he detects it. The *relation of means to ends* is for Collingwood the central characteristic of craft, and the following sums up his conception of craft: a craft is an activity in which some raw material is transformed by a learnable skill into a preconceived product. A work of craft is the product of this kind of activity. Shoemaking is a good example of craft; the shoemaker's skill and the leather are *means* to producing a specifiable and preconceived *end* (shoes).

Collingwood allows that craft and art can overlap so that the same thing can be a work of craft in one respect and a work of art in another respect. He also makes clear that an artist must master certain crafts as a prerequisite to communicating his art: a painter must know how to handle paints and the poet words so that their art (which is expression) can be made public. However, to have mastered such crafts does not make one an artist, and it is the mistake of the technical theory of art, according to Collingwood, that it does not realize this. What is the basis for Collingwood's claim that art (what he calls "art proper") and craft are completely different? He claims that he is simply making explicit how the word "art" is used in English. Collingwood's method in 1938 anticipates the "ordinary language" method popular among one wing of present-day analytic philosophers. He maintains that "art" has a number of senses in English and that when he describes "art proper" and distinguishes it from "art falsely so called," all users of English will recognize that his description marks out a usage of "art." He also assumes that it is this usage which underlies serious talk about art. His theory of art is, as he says, merely an attempt to tell us what we already know—because it is embedded in our language habits. We may not be able to formulate explicitly what we know in this sense, and Collingwood's aim is to help us so formulate it. He does not give arguments to support his view that art proper and craft are completely distinct; he assumes the distinction is correct and that all he has to do is to describe it and his reader will recognize its correctness. One can, however, think of the description as a kind of argument. The arguments he does give are subsequent to the art-craft distinction and presuppose the distinction.

Collingwood's first attempt to give a precise description of art proper involves trying to show that many of the things which are called "art" are *not* art proper. The two kinds of art falsely so called which he discusses are "amusement art" and "magical art." He characterizes amusement art as follows:

> If an artifact is designed to stimulate a certain emotion, and if this emotion is intended not for discharge into the occupations of ordinary life, but for enjoyment as something of value in itself, the function of the artifact is to amuse and entertain.[28]

He thinks ". . . that most of what generally goes by the name of art nowadays is not art at all, but amusement."[29] In preparing the way for his discussion of magical art, Collingwood, drawing on anthropological studies, presents a novel analysis of the concept of magic, the value of which is by no means limited to the theory of art. Although it is not the only kind of magical art, religious art is alleged to be a good example of it.

> Obviously its [religious art's] function is to evoke, and constantly re-evoke, certain emotions whose discharge is to be effected in the activities of everyday life. In calling it magical I am not denying its claim to the title religious.[30]

Patriotic monuments are also good examples of magical art; they evoke emotions which are useful for everyday life. Collingwood is careful to point out that amusement art is not necessarily bad, if it is used sparingly and is not mistaken for art proper. He also points out that magical art has an important role to play, as it is part of the ritual important to organized social life.

Amusement art and magical art have in common that they both are intended to *evoke* emotion. They differ in the role that the evoked emotions play. The emotions evoked by magical art are interwoven with the rest of life and act as motives for our everyday actions; for example, patriotic emotions motivate one to defend one's country. The emotions evoked by amusement art are ". . . intended to be earthed [grounded] instead of overflowing into the situations represented."[31] The situations represented by amusement art are "make-believe" and "unreal," and the emotions evoked are dissipated. Collingwood associates Aristotle's notion of catharsis with amusement art rather than with art proper.

Collingwood argues that amusement and magic are not art proper because they are forms of craft, it being taken for granted that art proper and craft are distinct. Amusement and magic are crafts because they are designed to evoke specific emotions which the maker of the artifact conceives of in advance. Collingwood thinks of the evoked emotions as products in the same way that shoes are the product of the craft of shoemaking. The amuser, the magician, and the shoemaker all have in mind a product they want to produce, and each has a technique for doing so.

Having analyzed amusement and magic in terms of evoked emotion, Collingwood assumes without argument that there is a necessary connection between art proper and emotion, although it is not a matter of evoking. (His assumption is perhaps explained by the fact that E. F. Carritt, a well-known expressionist, was Collingwood's tutor at Oxford. Collingwood may, for all his subtlety, be perpetuating without question a tradition he learned at school. Collingwood's theory is also strongly influenced by the Italian philosopher Croce.) The connection between art and emotion seems so obvious to Collingwood that he simply asserts it to be the case.

> Art has something to do with emotion; what it does with it has a certain resemblance to arousing it, but is not arousing it.[32]

> Since the artist proper has something to do with emotion, and what he does with it is not to arouse it, what is it that he does?[33]

His answer is that art *expresses* emotion rather than evokes it. Collingwood's argument may be reconstructed in the following way.

| | |
|---|---|
| 1. Art has something to do with emotion. | Assumption |
| 2. Art must either evoke emotion or express emotion; there are only two possibilities. | From 1 plus assumption about possibilities |
| 3. Art is not craft. | Previously proved |
| 4. Art cannot arouse emotion because if it did it would be craft. | From 2 and 3 |
| 5. Art is the expression of emotion. | From 2 and 4 |

The argument clearly depends on assumptions, and the acceptability of these will be examined later. The next task is to see what Collingwood means by "expresses emotion."

It is important to know what Collingwood means by "expresses emotion" because at this point he thinks that he has proved that art is identical with the expression of emotion and hence that an adequate description of the expression of emotion would also be an adequate theory of art. Emotion may be expressed in a number of ways—for example, by speech or by gesture. However, not every bodily movement involved with emotion is an expression of that emotion. A person may express his anger by saying, "You are an evil man." However, if a person says, "I am angry," he is not expressing his anger, he is denoting it. It is even more important for Collingwood not to confuse *betraying* emotion with expressing it. Care is required here, because we sometimes say, for example, that distortions of the face express pain and that turning pale and stammering express fear. These bodily phenomena are significantly different from other activities that are said to be expressions, and Collingwood marks the differences by saying that these are *betrayals* of emotion. Betrayals are uncontrolled reactions, and Collingwood presumably thinks that such reactions cannot be identified with art. The kinds of occurrences which we call "expressions" and which Collingwood wants to identify with art are those which are ". . . under our control and are conceived by us, in our awareness of controlling them, as our way of expressing these emotions . . ."[34] The important differences, then, between betraying and expressing emotion are *control* and *awareness of control*: distortion of the face when in pain is not controlled, nor need one be aware that one's face is distorted. The same may be said of stammering, turning pale, and so on. Late in his book, Collingwood says that betrayals are a primitive form of expression and designates them "psychical expressions,"[35] but this is done to distinguish them from what might be called "expression proper." Consciously controlled expression of emotion is, Collingwood says, *language*—language in a broad sense which "... includes any activity of any organ which is expressive in the same way in which speech is expressive."[36] "Art must be language."[37] Collingwood concludes that "the expressing of emotion," "art proper," and "language" all refer to the same thing: expression = art = language.

It is perhaps implicit in what has already been said, but there is a feature of Collingwood's conception of expressing emotion which needs to be made completely explicit because it has such far-reaching consequences for his conception of art. He makes his point in this frequently quoted passage in which he describes what happens when someone expresses emotion.

> At first, he is conscious of having an emotion, but not conscious of what this emotion is. All he is conscious of is a perturbation or excitement, which he feels going on within him, but of whose nature he is ignorant. While in this state, all he can say about his emotion is: 'I feel ... I don't know what I feel.' From this helpless and oppressed condition he extricates himself by doing something which we call expressing himself. . . . he expresses himself by speaking. . . . the emotion expressed is an emotion of whose nature the person who feels it is no longer unconscious.[38]

This passage makes it clear that expressing emotion involves the expresser's explicit knowledge of the *specific* emotion which is expressed. When Collingwood speaks of specific emotion, he does not mean simply fear, anger, and so on, but the specific *kind* of anger, fear, and so on. It follows from this analysis of expressing emotion that it cannot be known ahead of time that a specific emotion will be expressed or what, if any, emotion will be expressed. The nature of an expressed emotion cannot be known until it has been expressed. Since art has been identified with expressing emotion, this means that an artist cannot know ahead of time what he will create. Collingwood presses this point very hard. He does not simply mean that an artist cannot know in complete detail what he will do. "No artist . . . can set out to write a comedy, a tragedy, an elegy, or the like. So far as he is an artist proper, he is just as likely to write any one of these as any other . . ."[39] Collingwood is not simply claiming the obvious, namely, that an artist might start out to write, say, a comedy and end up with a tragedy, for he says an artist proper is "just as likely to write any of these as any other." Readers may assume there must be many counterexamples to this statement, but Collingwood tries to neutralize these examples by classifying them as amusement or magic art. The amusement and magic artists know ahead of time what they want to produce and have the means to do so, and this is why their works are not art, but craft. Collingwood is very bold about what he classifies as craft: at one point, he suggests that the plays of Shakespeare are not art because they were designed to please (evoke emotion in) Elizabethan audiences.[40]

This is a startling conclusion, for most people would consider Shakespeare's plays to be paradigms of works of art. And there is a further question: how can someone other than the artist himself know that his work expresses emotion? Collingwood's answer is that "we know that he [the artist] is expressing his emotions by the fact that he is enabling us to express ours."[41] This answer suffices for some cases, but what of the cases in which, say, a poet has in fact expressed his emotion but the reader for some reason is unable to realize this fact? In such cases, the reader will not be able to tell whether the work is craft or art. Collingwood's reading of Shakespeare may be a case in point. Perhaps Shakespeare's words do not "work" for Collingwood and he has therefore concluded that they must have been designed to evoke emotion and are craft. This point at least brings out that Collingwood's criterion of art proper is difficult to apply.

Thus far, only the expressive aspect of Collingwood's theory of art has been discussed, but he thinks the definition of art also involves another aspect—imagination. In order for something to be art, it must be *both* expressive and imaginative.[42] Collingwood's use of imagination has come in for a great deal of adverse criticism. Alan Donagan, in an otherwise sympathetic treatment of Collingwood's theory of art, claims that Collingwood confuses two distinct senses of "to imagine" and as a result draws a false conclusion.[43] The two senses are 1) the act of forming mental images and 2) the act of bringing something into consciousness or awareness. Collingwood is correct when he concludes that a work of art *may* be imaginary in the first sense; for example, a poet might create a poem by saying some words to himself, and the poem would be only, to use Collingwood's phrase, "in his head." Let it be assumed that Collingwood is also right in thinking that *all* works of art are imaginary in the second sense, namely that they are the result of bringing something into consciousness. Nothing about bringing something into consciousness requires that the thing so brought is necessarily "in the head" only. For example, when an artist paints on a canvas, he brings something, say, the representation of a woman, into consciousness, but the representation is a public object and not in the head only. The second sense of "to imagine" appears to be identical with what Collingwood means by "to express," so that to say that works of art are expressions *and* imaginary in the second sense is redundant. In any event, Collingwood appears to have confused his two senses of "to imagine" and to have drawn the conclusion that *all* works of art are imaginary in the sense of being in the head only. Consequently, he denies that such public objects as statues, paintings, and the like are works of art. He claims that the only real works of art are the mental images formed in the mind of the artist before or as he creates a public object or the mental images formed in the mind of the spectator as the result of experiencing a public object. This conclusion is especially strange for a philosopher who purports to be following ordinary usage.

Collingwood tries to deduce criteria of good and bad art

from his definition of art. He begins his discussion of the evaluation of art with the remark that "The definition of any given kind of thing is also the definition of a good thing of that kind . . ."[44] But surely this is not true. Consider a dictionary definition of "goat" which reads, "Any of certain hollow-horned ruminant mammals allied to the sheep, but of lighter build, with backwardly arching horns, a short tail, and (usually) straight hair."[45] An animal might satisfy all of the criteria mentioned in this definition and still be a very poor goat. For example, he might have backwardly arching horns but they might be very short, or he might be chronically ill, and so on. Collingwood confuses the classification of a thing as a thing of a certain kind with the question of whether a thing is a good thing of its kind. If he were right, every goat would be a good goat, every man a good man, and every work of art a good work of art. We do, however, frequently speak of bad works of art. Collingwood tries to account for this by saying that "A bad work of art is an activity in which the agent tries to express a given emotion, but fails."[46] In other words, a bad work of art is something which tried to be a work of art but failed. The most obvious difficulty is the paradox that a bad work of art turns out not to be a work of art! One would think that for something to be a bad thing of a certain type, it would have to be of that type —a bad horse would have to be a horse to begin with. Also, Collingwood's evaluational scheme is so simple that it cannot account for some cases of bad art. For example, someone might write a poem which in fact expresses his emotion without any preconceived plan of evoking emotion, and it might still be a bad poem.

It is now time to examine some of Collingwood's assumptions and conclusions. First, it is not at all clear that art *necessarily* "has something to do with emotion." One can think of many nonobjective paintings and pieces of music which are not expressive of emotion (or perhaps of anything else). If Collingwood were to try to answer this criticism by saying that such things are not works of art, he would be in the difficult position of maintaining that things which ordinary usage calls works of art are not art. However, the answer that Collingwood would probably try to give the present criticism is that all expression involves emotion. This emerges when he gives an analysis of discourse, or speech.

> . . . it is a matter of fact that discourse in which a determined attempt is made to state truths retains an element of emotional expressiveness. No serious writer or speaker ever utters a thought unless he thinks it worth uttering.[47]

Presumably he thinks the same holds for painting, sculpting, and the like as well as for the literary arts. However, the concept of emotion is stretched so thin here that it becomes meaningless. When I say to my child, "Go brush your teeth," I always think it worth saying, but the remark is not always expressive of emotion. On some occasions, I am merely reminding him and no emotion is involved; on other occasions, when he offers resistance, emotion becomes involved and is usually expressed by the same remark uttered in a loud tone of voice. It simply is not true that every important remark expresses emotion, and Collingwood's attempt to ensure the presence of emotion only succeeds in emptying the concept of emotion of content. The point of this criticism is that the expression of emotion is not a *necessary* condition of art.

Another difficulty is that Collingwood's definition classifies as works of art an enormously large number of things which no one has the least inclination to think of as works of art. For example, "Go brush your teeth" said in a way which expresses emotion (exasperation) would be a work of art, presumably a poem, if the remark were not intended to evoke emotion. The theory is clearly much too broad. Collingwood's theory has the curious quality of being both too narrow and too broad. It claims that the plays of Shakespeare and many other works are entertainment and not works of art, and it rules out many other works as magic. Any theory which rules out the very paradigms of art is too narrow and hence defective.

One flaw in Collingwood's theory is that he mixes up two distinct senses of "work of art," both of which are sanctioned by ordinary usage—the classificatory and the evaluative senses. Earlier I illustrated the latter sense with the remark, "This painting is a work of art." Here the expression "work of art" is being used to say that the subject of the sentence is good or perhaps even magnificent. Unless the expression is being used evaluatively, it is redundant because the expression "This painting" establishes that the object referred to is a work of art in the classificatory sense. The classificatory sense is illustrated by a remark such as "This is a work of art," when the sentence is used to tell someone that a design is a work of art and not simply a product of nature, that a pile of metal is a work of art and not discarded junk, or that an object dug from the earth on an archaeological site is a work of art and not a stone. The evaluative sense is probably used much more frequently, because there are not many occasions on which we need to use the classificatory sense in ordinary discourse. However, even if we do not frequently employ the classificatory sense in speech, it is embedded in our thought and plays an important role in the way we conceive the world around us. One way to show the existence and importance of the classificatory sense is to reflect on the fact that we frequently say that a work of art is bad; we could not do this if we were using only the evaluative sense. An adequate theory of art must distinguish these two senses of the term and give a coherent account of them. Such an account will be attempted in Chapter 11.

At the end of his book, Collingwood discusses what is apparently for him one of the paradigms of art, T. S. Eliot's "The Waste Land." With this poem in mind, he speaks of the role of the artist.

> His business as an artist is to speak out, to make a clean breast. But what he has to utter is not, as the individualist theory of art would have us think, his own secrets. As spokesmen of his community, the secrets he must utter are theirs.[48]

These final remarks reveal the motive behind his theory—to give an account of what might be best called "serious art." He calls it "art proper." If he had originally conceived of serious art, entertainment art, and magical art as three aspects of art, he would have been off to a better start. Even so, there would still be many difficulties in his theory. Collingwood is, however, making an important point about what art can do—it can reveal secrets and it can be expressive—but he is wrong in thinking that all art does this. He seizes on an important aspect of art but makes the mistake of thinking that that aspect is all there is to art. Instead of a theory of art, Collingwood has a theory of an aspect of art.

Each of the three philosophies of art discussed thus far has offered a definition of art, and in each case the definition has been specified in terms of characteristics which all works of art allegedly have in common: significant form, forms symbolic of human feeling, and the expression of emotion. The Wittgensteinian philosophy of art which will be discussed in the next section strongly challenges the traditional demand that works of art have something in common, *an essence,* which if discovered will serve as the defining characteristic of art.

---

## Chapter 10. Art as an Open Concept

---

IN PART II the influence of Wittgenstein on the concept of aesthetic object was indicated, but his work on what has come to be known as the notion of *open concept* has had an even greater influence on the theory of art. An open concept is a concept for which there is no necessary condition in order for something to be an instance of that concept. Dugald Stewart's analysis of beauty—discussed in Chapter 2—was an attempt to show that beauty is an open concept. Wittgenstein's frequently quoted example is that of *game.* He maintains that if we consider the whole range of games, say, from football to solitaire, we will not be able to discover any characteristic which is common to every game, and thus that there is no characteristic necessary for something to be a game. Wittgenstein's point is that many, and perhaps even most, concepts are *open* and that philosophers have frequently been mistaken in trying to specify definitions for concepts in terms of necessary and sufficient conditions. It should be noted that Wittgenstein was not saying that there is anything wrong with open concepts, but simply that some concepts are open and that philosophers ought to take it into account in developing their theories.

In a well-known and widely reprinted article,[49] Morris Weitz tries to adapt Wittgenstein's thesis to the theory of art, arguing that art is an open concept. In stating his argument, Weitz makes the very important distinction between the generic concept of art and the subconcepts of art. Weitz's argument consists of 1) an argument which purports to show that a subconcept of art, the novel, is an open concept and 2) the contention that all other subconcepts of art and the generic concept of art itself are open too. He says a consideration of such a question as "Is Dos Passos's *U.S.A.* a novel?" will show that the novel is an open concept. *U.S.A.* has certain features in common with other novels but has no regular time sequence and is interspersed with actual newspaper stories, and, of course, it is just these novelties which cause some people to question whether or not it is a novel. Weitz maintains that if we look at works which are unquestionably called "novels," we will find similar differences. He is suggesting that the class of novels is like the class of games, that is, the class of games as conceived by Wittgenstein. He then generalizes:

> What is true of the novel is, I think, true of every sub-concept of art: "tragedy," "comedy," "painting," "opera," etc., of "art" itself. No "Is X a novel, painting, opera, work of art, etc.?" question allows of a definitive answer in the sense of a factual yes or no report.[50]

According to Weitz, all the members of a subconcept of art —for example, tragedy—may not have a feature in common. Tragedy *A* and tragedy *B* may have features in common, tragedy *B* and tragedy *C* may also, and so on, but tragedy *A* and tragedy *Z* may not. Weitz's view is that the tragedies have "family resemblances" among themselves but no common feature. It is, of course, possible in his view for all the members of a species of art to have a feature in common *at a given time,* but his main point is that it is all but inevitable that some new work will be created which resembles many of the members of the subconcept but lacks the common feature. Weitz claims that when this kind of thing happens the new work is typically included within the subconcept despite its lack of the common feature and this shows that the subconcept is an open concept. He thinks the same holds for the generic concept of art. To show how far Weitz pushes his thesis, it may be noted that he maintains that "being an artifact" is not a necessary condition for the generic sense of "art." His reason is that we sometimes utter such statements as "This piece of driftwood is a lovely piece of sculpture." He reasons that if we are willing to classify a piece of driftwood as sculpture, i.e., as a work of art, then artifactuality cannot be a necessary condition of art.

In addition to his thesis about the nature of the concepts of art, Weitz also maintains that, if we choose, we can close a concept by specifying a necessary condition or conditions and sticking to it or them. However, he warns that to do so "is ludicrous since it forecloses on the very conditions of creativity in the arts."[51]

For a long time Weitz's view seemed incontrovertible. Its relation to Wittgenstein lent it great prestige, and while not everyone found the argument persuasive and some attacked it, the conclusion did seem right to a very large number of philosophers. Recently, however, Maurice Mandelbaum has challenged both Wittgenstein's argument about games and Weitz's argument about art in a most interesting way. He argues that games have in common a certain kind of purpose: "the potentiality of . . . [an] absorbing non-practical interest to either participants or spectators."[52] Wittgenstein failed to notice this feature because he was apparently concerned only with *exhibited* characteristics such as whether a ball was used in the game or whether the game could be won and lost. Mandelbaum does not attempt to define art or its subconcepts, but he does make the acute suggestion that art may be definable in terms of some *nonexhibited* character-istics, perhaps in terms of some relational features which relate an object to "some actual or possible audience."[53]

---

## Chapter 11.  Art as a Social Institution

---

IN WHAT FOLLOWS it is maintained that Weitz is wrong and that the generic sense of "art" can be defined, although it is admitted that he may be right to the extent that all or some of the subconcepts of art such as novel, tragedy, ceramics, sculpture, painting, etc., may lack necessary conditions *for their application as subconcepts.*[54] For example, there may not be any characteristics common to all tragedies which would distinguish them from comedies, satyr plays, happen-ings, and the like *within the domain of art,* but it may be that there are characteristics which works of art have which would distinguish them from nonart.

The first obstacle to defining art is Weitz's contention that artifactuality is not a necessary condition for art. Most people assume that there is a sharp distinction between works of art and natural objects, but Weitz has argued that the fact that we sometimes say of natural objects such as driftwood that they are works of art breaks down the distinction. In short, there appear to be works of art which are not arti-facts. However, Weitz's argument is inconclusive because he fails to take account of the two senses of "work of art"—the evaluative and classificatory. The application of this dis-tinction to the problem at hand requires some expansion of the remarks in Chapter 10 and also involves some repetition.

There is a certain irony here because Weitz makes the distinction in his article, but he does not see that it undercuts his own argument. The evaluative sense of "work of art" is used to praise an object—for example, "That driftwood is a work of art" or "That painting is a work of art." In these examples we are saying that the driftwood and the painting have qualities worthy of notice and praise. In neither case do we mean that the object referred to by the subject of the sentence is a work of art in the classificatory sense: we are speaking evaluatively about the driftwood and the painting. It would be silly to take "That painting is a work of art" as a classificatory statement; ordinarily to utter the expression "That painting" is to commit oneself to meaning that the referent of the expression is a work of art. The classificatory sense is used simply to indicate that a thing belongs to a certain category of artifacts. We rarely utter sentences in which we use the classificatory sense because it is such a basic notion. We are rarely in situations in which it is necessary to raise the question of whether or not an object is a work of art in the classificatory sense. We generally know straight away whether or not an object is a work of art. Generally, no one needs to say, by way of classification, "That is a work of art." However, recent developments in art such as junk sculpture and found art may occasionally force such remarks. For example, I was recently in a room at the Museum of Modern Art in which a work of art consisting of 144 one-foot-square metal plates was spread out on the floor. A man walked through the room and right across the work of art, apparently without seeing it. I did not, but I could have said, "Do you know that you are walking across a work of art?" The point is that the classificatory sense of "work of art" is a basic concept which structures and guides our thinking about our world. The whole point can perhaps be made clear by considering what would happen if one tried to understand the sentence "That painting is a work of art" in the classificatory sense. As indicated above, the expression "That painting" already contains the information that the object referred to is a work of art. Consequently, if the expression "That painting" is replaced in the sentence with its approximate equivalent, "That work of art which was created by putting paint on a surface such as canvas," the resulting sentence would be "That work of art which was created by putting paint on a surface such as canvas is a work of art." Thus, if one tries to understand this sentence by taking the last occurrence of "work of art" in the classificatory sense, the whole sentence turns into a tautology; that is, it is redundant. However, one would scarcely utter "That painting is a work of art" meaning to utter a tautology, that is, simply to say that a work of art in the classificatory sense is a work of art in the classificatory sense. It is clear that what would generally be meant by such a sentence about a painting is that a work of art in the classificatory sense is a work of art in the evaluative sense. A parallel analysis could be given for the sentence about the driftwood, except that if one tried to understand "That piece of driftwood is a work of art" by construing "work of art" in the classificatory sense, a contradiction would result rather than a redundancy. It is, however, easy to understand this sentence construing "work of art" in the evaluative sense.

Weitz's conclusion that *being an artifact* is not a necessary condition for being a work of art rests upon a confusion. What his argument proves is that it is not necessary for an object to be an artifact in order to be called (quite correctly) a work of art, when this expression is understood in the evaluative sense. It is, by the way, not at all surprising that the members of the class of objects which we find worthy of notice and praise do not all have a characteristic in common. Such a class would naturally be large and varied. Once we grasp the significance of the *two* senses of "work of art" and see that Weitz's argument is misleading, we are free to reflect clearly on our understanding of the classificatory sense. And surely when we do so reflect, we realize that *part* of what is meant when we think of or assert of something (not in praise) that it is a work of art is that it is an artifact. The remainder of what is meant by the classificatory sense of "work of art" is the concern of the rest of this chapter. However, before going on to that task, it is worth noting that the property of artifactuality is not an *exhibited* property, or at least usually is not. Mandelbaum accused Wittgenstein of neglecting nonexhibited properties and Weitz also neglects them. The point is that artifactuality, unlike such properties as color, shape, and size, is not exhibited when the artifact is observed, except in those infrequent cases in which the act of creation of the artifact is observed. Artifactuality is a relational, nonexhibited property, and perhaps this is also true of the other property or properties which distinguish art from nonart and which are involved in the definition of art.

Although he does not try to formulate a definition of art, Arthur Danto in his provocative article, "The Artworld,"[55] draws conclusions which suggest the direction such attempts at definition must take. In reflecting upon art and its history in general and such present-day developments as Warhol's "Brillo Carton" and Rauschenberg's "Bed" in particular, Danto writes, "To see something as art requires something the eye cannot descry—an atmosphere of artistic theory, a knowledge of history of art: an artworld."[56] Danto seems to agree with Mandelbaum about the importance of non-exhibited properties (what the eye cannot descry), but he perhaps goes further than Mandelbaum by speaking provocatively, if vaguely, of atmosphere and history—of an artworld. Perhaps the substance of Danto's remark can be captured in a formal definition. The definition will first be formulated and then its implications and adequacy will be examined.

A work of art in the classificatory sense is 1) an artifact 2) upon which some person or persons acting on behalf of a certain social institution (the artworld) has conferred the status of candidate for appreciation.

The definition speaks of conferring status and what is involved in this must be made clear. The most obvious and clear-cut examples of the conferring of status are certain actions of the state in which legal status is involved. A king's conferring of knighthood, a grand jury's indicting someone, the chairman of the election board certifying that someone is a candidate for office, or a minister pronouncing a couple man and wife are examples in which a person acting on behalf of a social institution (the state) confers *legal* status. These examples suggest that pomp and ceremony are required to establish a legal status; but this is not so. For example, in some jurisdictions common-law marriage is possible—a legal status acquired without ceremony.

The conferring of a Ph.D. degree on someone by a university, the election of someone as president of the Rotary, and the declaring of an object as a relic of the church are examples in which a person or persons confer nonlegal status. As before, ceremony is not required to establish this kind of status; for example, a person can acquire without ceremony the status of wise man within a community. What the offered definition of a work of art suggests is that just as a person can be certified as a candidate for office or two persons can acquire the status of common-law marriage within a legal system and as a person can be elected president of the Rotary or a person can acquire the status of wise man within a community, an artifact can acquire the status of candidate for appreciation within the social system which Danto has called "the artworld."

Two questions arise about the *conferring* of the status of candidate for appreciation: how does one know when the status has been conferred, and how is it conferred? An artifact's hanging in an art museum as part of a show or a performance at a theater are sure signs that the status has been conferred; these are paradigm cases of knowing that the status has been conferred. There is, of course, no guarantee that one can always know whether something is a candidate for appreciation, just as one cannot always tell that a given person is a knight or is married. The second question of how the status is conferred is the more important of the two questions, however. The examples mentioned—hanging in a museum and a performance in a theater—seems to suggest that a number of persons is required for the actual conferring of the status in question. In one sense, a number of persons is required, and in another sense, only one person is required. A number of persons are required to make up the social institution of the artworld, but only one person is required to act on behalf of or as an agent of the artworld and to confer the status of candidate for appreciation. Many works of art are never seen by anyone but the persons who create them, but they are still works of art. The status in question may be acquired by *a single person's treating an artifact as a candidate for appreciation.* Of course nothing prevents a group of persons conferring the status, but it is usually conferred by a single person, the artist who creates the artifact.

It may be helpful to compare and contrast the notion of conferring the status of candidate for appreciation with a case in which something is simply presented for appreciation; this device may throw light on the notion of conferring the status of candidate. Consider the case of a salesman of plumbing supplies who spreads his wares before us. There is an important difference between "placing before" and "conferring the status of candidate," and this difference can be brought out by comparing the salesman's action with the superficially similar act of Duchamp in entering a urinal which he christened "Fountain" in that now famous art show. The difference is that Duchamp's action took place within the institutional setting of the artworld, and the plumbing salesman's action took place outside of it. The salesman could do what Duchamp did, that is, convert a urinal into a work of art, but such a thing probably would not occur to him. Please remember that calling "Fountain" a work of art does not mean that it is a good one, nor does this qualification insinuate that it is a bad one either.

It may be felt that the notion of conferring status within the artworld is excessively vague. Certainly this notion is not as clear-cut as is the conferring of status within the legal system, where procedures and lines of authority are explicitly defined and incorporated into law. The counterparts in the artworld to specified procedures and lines of authority are nowhere codified, and the artworld carries on its business at the level of customary practice. Still there *is* a practice and this defines a social institution. A social institution need not have a formally established constitution, officers, and bylaws in order to exist and have the capacity to confer status. Some social institutions are formal and some are informal. The artworld could become formalized, but most people who are interested in art would probably consider this a bad thing: Such formality would threaten the freshness and exuberance of art. Every person who sees himself as a member of the artworld is an "officer" of it and is thereby capable of conferring status in its name. One present-day artist has in the case of one of his works even gone through the motions —no doubt as a burlesque—of using a formal procedure characteristic of many legal and some nonlegal institutions. Walter de Maria's "High Energy Bar," which is a stainless-steel bar, is accompanied by a certificate which bears the name of the work and states that the bar is a work of art only when the certificate is present. This amusing example serves to suggest the significance of the act of naming works of art. An object may acquire the status of art without ever being named, but giving it a title makes clear to whomever is interested that an object is a work of art. Specific titles function in a variety of ways—for example, as aids in understanding a work or as a convenient way of identifying a work—but any title at all (even the name "Untitled") is a badge of status.

Let us now pass on to a discussion of the notion of appreciation. Notice that the definition speaks of the conferring of the status of *candidate* for appreciation. Nothing is said about actual appreciation, and this leaves open the possibility for works of art which, for whatever reason, are not appreciated. It is important not to build into the definition of the classificatory sense of "work of art" value properties such as actual appreciation: to do so would make it impossible to speak of unappreciated works of art and of bad works of art, and this is clearly undesirable. Any theory of art must preserve certain central features of the way in which we talk about art, and we do find it necessary sometimes to speak of bad art. It should also be noted that not every aspect of a work of art is included in the candidacy for appreciation. For example, the color of the back of a painting is not ordinarily an object of appreciation. The reader will recognize that the question of which aspects of a work of art are to be included within the candidacy for appreciation has already been dealt with in Part II.

The definition of art given above ought for the sake of completeness to include a qualification about the various aspects of works of art, but such a qualification would make the definition unduly complicated and the reader should understand the definition with the qualification in mind.

There is a second consideration about appreciation which must be brought out in order to counter the suspicion which may arise in the minds of some that the definition depends on there being special kind of aesthetic appreciation. In Part II it was argued that there is no special kind of aesthetic perception and, similarly, that there does not seem to be any reason to think that a special kind of aesthetic appreciation exists. All that is meant by "appreciation" in the definition is something like "in experiencing the qualities of a thing one finds them worthy or valuable," and this meaning applies quite generally both inside and outside the domain of art.

The institutional theory of art which is set forth here has quite consciously been worked out with the practices of the artworld in mind—especially developments of the last seventy-five years, such as dadaism, pop art, found art, and happenings. The institutional theory and these developments raise a number of questions, and a few of these will be dealt with here.

First, if Duchamp can convert a urinal, a snowshovel, and a hatrack into works of art, can't natural objects such as driftwood also become works of art? Such natural objects can become works of art if any one of a number of things is done to them. One thing which would do the trick would be to pick a natural object up, take it home, and hang it on the wall. Another thing would be to pick it up and enter it in an exhibition. It was being assumed earlier that Weitz's sentence about the driftwood referred to a piece of driftwood in its ordinary situation on a beach and untouched by human hand. Please keep in mind that for something to be a work of art in the classificatory sense does not mean that it has any actual value. Natural objects which become works of art in the way being discussed are artifactualized without the use of tools—the artifactuality is conferred on the object rather than worked on it.

Second, a question which frequently arises in connection with discussions of the concept of art and which seems especially relevant in the context of institutional theory is, "How are we to conceive of paintings done by individuals such as Betsy the chimpanzee from the Baltimore Zoo?" Calling Betsy's products "paintings" here is not meant to prejudge that they are works of art; it is just that some word is needed to refer to them. The question of whether or not Betsy's paintings are art depends on what is done with them. For example, a year or two ago The Field Museum of Natural History in Chicago exhibited some chimpanzee and gorilla paintings. In the case of these paintings we must say that they are not works of art. However, if they had been exhibited a few miles away at the Chicago Art Institute they would have been works of art—the paintings would have been art if the director of the Art Institute had, so to speak, gone out on a limb. It all depends on the institutional setting—the one setting is congenial to conferring the status of art and the other is not. What would make Betsy's paintings works of art would be some agent's conferring the status on behalf of the artworld. Despite the fact that Betsy did the painting, the resulting works of art would not be Betsy's but the work of the person who does the conferring. Betsy cannot do the conferring because she cannot see herself as an agent of the artworld—she is unable to participate (fully) in our culture.

Weitz's charge that the defining of art or its subconcepts forecloses creativity requires discussion. Some of the traditional definitions of art may have and some of the traditional definitions of its subconcepts probably did foreclose creativity, but the institutional definition of art certainly will not. The requirement of artifactuality can scarcely prevent creativity, since artifactuality is a necessary condition of creativity. How could there be an instance of creativity without an artifact of some kind being produced? The other requirement involving the conferring of status could not inhibit creativity; in fact, it encourages it. Since it is possible that anything whatever may become art, the definition imposes no restraints on creativity. Weitz is probably right that the definition of some of the subconcepts of art have foreclosed creativity, but this danger is now a thing of the past. In the past, it may very well have happened that, for example, a playwright conceived of and wished to write a play with tragic features but which lacked a defining characteristic of, say, Aristotle's definition of tragedy. Faced with this dilemma, the playwright might have been intimidated and put his project aside. However, with the present-day disregard for established genres and the clamor for novelty in art, this obstacle to creativity probably no longer exists. Today, if a new and unusual work is created and it is fairly similar to some members of an established type, then it will usually be accommodated within that type, or if the new work is very unlike any existing works, then a new subconcept will probably be created. Artists today are not easily intimidated, and they regard art genres as loose guidelines rather than as rigid specification.

The institutional theory of art may sound like saying, "A work of art is an object of which someone has said, 'I christen this object a work of art.'" And it is rather like that; although this does not mean that the conferring of the status of art is a simple matter. Just as christening a child has as its background the history and structure of the church, conferring the status of art has as its background the Byzantine complexity of the artworld. Some persons may find it strange that in the nonart cases discussed it appears that there are ways in which the conferring can go wrong, while there does not appear to be a way in which conferring the status of art can be invalid. For example, a king might say the wrong words or use the wrong instrument and the person who was to be knighted would not be a knight; or an indictment might have been improperly drawn up, and the person charged would not actually be indicted. But nothing parallel seems possible in the case of art. This fact reflects the differences between the artworld and legal institutions. The legal system deals with matters of grave personal consequences and its procedures must reflect this; the artworld deals with important matters also, but they are of a different sort entirely. The artworld does not require rigid procedures; it admits and even encourages frivolity and caprice without losing its serious purpose. However, if it is not possible to make a mistake *in* conferring the status of art, it is possible to make a mistake *by* conferring it. In conferring the status of art on an object one assumes a certain kind of responsibility for the object in its new status; presenting a candidate for appreciation always faces the possibility that no one will appreciate it and that the person who did the conferring will thereby lose face. One *can* make a work of art out of a sow's ear, but that does not necessarily make it a silk purse.

# PART IV

# Four Problems in Aesthetics

The core notions of beauty, art, and the aesthetic have been the focus of the previous chapters. These ideas organize and define the field of aesthetics. However, the philosophical problems generated by our thinking and talking about art are many and varied. This chapter will be devoted to discussing some noncore problems of aesthetics. Some of them are closely related to the core questions and some are not; the relation of others to the core is unclear and awaits clarification. The terms "core" and "noncore" should not be taken as indicating the importance or urgency of the problems so designated. The attempt to discover a core for aesthetics is an attempt to provide stability and organization for what is by common agreement an untidy discipline. The core provides a framework for orientation which gives us a sense of where we are as we work on the problems of aesthetics.

From the large number of noncore questions, I have selected four. There are 1) intentionalist criticism, 2) symbolism in art, 3) metaphor, and 4) expression. With the exception of metaphor, which involves only the literary arts, these questions cut across all of the arts. Each of the four has long been regarded by philosophers and critics as a most important question. Why they have been so regarded will, I think, emerge in the following discussions.

## Chapter 12.  Intentionalist Criticism

It is an undeniable fact that an artist always has some intention or other when he creates a work of art, even when the work is a case of "accidental art." A painter intends or hopes to produce a certain kind of effect—luminosity, perhaps— or to represent a woman or a landscape. A composer intends to create a musical score which when performed will result in music that is majestic, gay, solemn, or has some other musical qualities. A poet intends a line or a whole poem to express a certain meaning, for example, his love or a revolutionary message. In the case of accidental art, the result is intentional in the sense that the artist intentionally leaves the result unrevised. Many critics explicitly claim or assume that the artist's intention has an important role to play in criticism. The philosophical problem is to inquire whether or not the claim of the intentionalist critics is justified. In this section, intentionalist criticism will be analyzed, and an attempt will be made to show that it is fundamentally misguided.

Intentionalist critics do not agree about the significance of the intention of the artist. Some critics think that the artist's intention is important *both* for understanding a work of art and for evaluating a work, while others deny the significance of the intention for evaluation. However, before criticizing intentionalism, let us consider some generalized examples of intentionalist criticism.[1] According to an intentionalist critic, a painting must be taken as representing, say, a king because the painter intended it to represent a king. Suppose that the painting in question is an abstract painting and it is difficult to make out what, if anything, is represented in the painting. An intentionalist critic would try to settle a dispute about what is represented in the painting by appealing to the intention of the painter. Or suppose the question is that of the meaning of a difficult line in a poem—difficult either because it is obscure or because it is ambiguous. Again an intentionalist critic will try to discover the meaning of the line by reference to the poet's intention. A somewhat more complicated but logically similar situation obtains with those arts in which performance is involved. An intentionalist critic will demand that a play be performed according to the explicit stage directions of the playwright, or if stage directions are lacking, according to the intention of the playwright discoverable in some other way. Similarly, a musical score ought to be performed as the composer intended. These cases involve either the understanding of some work or the establishing of a correct performance.

The attempt to use the intention of the artist as a criterion of *evaluation* is different from the question of how the artist's intention relates to understanding or correct performance. Simply put, this intentionalist claim is that a work of art is good if its creator has succeeded in achieving what he intended to realize or bad to the extent that he fails to realize his intention. The evaluative use of the artist's intention faces a number of difficulties which will be discussed later, but there are two difficulties which so transparently undermine it that they should be discussed immediately. The first difficulty is a practical one, namely that it frequently is not possible to discover what an artist's intention was, so one cannot know if the intention has been realized or not. Shakespeare is a good example here; nothing is known of what his intentions were. Therefore, insofar as the artist's intention is necessary for evaluation, Shakespeare's plays cannot be evaluated. Of course, the intentionalist need not say that the artist's intention is the *only* criterion for evaluation, even though he clearly wants to maintain that it is a prime one. The second difficulty is more theoretical in nature. An artist might have very modest intentions and as a result always realize his intentions: does that mean his work is always good? An artist might have extremely ambitious intentions and as a result never realize his intentions: does that mean his work is always bad? These considerations conclusively show that success in realizing intentions cannot be used as a criterion of the value of a work of art. As Beardsley has noted, an artist's success in realizing his intentions is at best a criterion of how good the artist is in carrying out what he wants to do.[2] The worth of a work of art itself must clearly be established in some other way.

Unfortunately, the question of the relation of the artist's intention to an understanding of the *meaning* of a work of art or some part of a work cannot be dealt with so easily. "Meaning" is being used here to include such things as representation in the graphic arts and the meaning of a poetic line. The artist's intention and poetic meaning will be discussed in considerable detail, then an attempt will be made to show that the conclusion of this discussion can be construed generally for the various arts. An attempt will also be made to show how the generalized conclusion applies to the problem of correct performance.

Perhaps the simplest and quickest way to show that a poet's intention is independent of the meaning of his poetic lines is to consider computer poems. To produce computer poems, a computer must be programmed with a vocabulary, punctuation marks, spaces to separate words, and so on, which the computer randomly combines in a large variety of ways. Most of the combinations produced will be nonsense, but sooner or later the computer will type out,

> The cat is on the mat.
> The cat is very fat.

The meaning of this simple and uninteresting poem (the value of poems is not an issue now, only what they mean) is evident to anyone who understands English. However, no intention was involved in the production of the poem, because the computer used does not have intentions. Of course, intentions are involved in the programming of the computer —a particular vocabulary is put into it and so on—but the computer puts the words together in a random manner, and no programmer's intention can be responsible for the word sequences produced.

If the significance of this example is fully grasped, the reader will see the independence of meaning and intention. However, someone might think that the cat poem is a special case because it is so unambiguous and simple and might raise the question about the poet's intention when poems are difficult and obscure. To meet this possible objection, I shall turn to a general discussion of language use, meaning, and intention. Given vocabulary enough and time, however, a computer would type out every poem ever written without intending anything.

Let me take ambiguous sentences as the test case. A sentence is ambiguous when it is possible to construe it to have two or more different meanings. Examples of ambiguous sentences are, "I like my secretary better than my wife," and the line from an old hymn, ". . . the sounds I hear falling on my ear . . ." The former may be understood to mean either "I like my secretary better than my wife likes my secretary" or "I like my secretary better than I like my wife." The latter may be understood to mean either "I hear sounds which fall on my ear" or "I hear sounds at the same time that I fall on my ear (fall down)." The intentionalist critic maintains the ambiguity in poetic lines can be cleared up by discovering what the poet intended. If a sentence can be construed to mean *A* or *B* and the poet meant *A*, then the sentence means *A*.

The intentionalists' misconception about ambiguity can be revealed by reflecting on the relation between a word sequence or sentence and the various kinds of conditions under which the sentence can be uttered.

Although ambiguous word sequences are sometimes uttered, sentences are not typically ambiguous; if they were typically ambiguous, communication would be impossible. Sometimes the nonlinguistic conditions in which a sentence is uttered make the sentence unambiguous, as when someone says "I saw her duck" in the presence of a group which contains a young lady who has just ducked her head and no member of the family Anatidae is or has been present. Sometimes the other sentences which occur in the same discourse are sufficient to make a given sentence unambiguous, as when "I saw her duck" is immediately followed by "and its feathers were black and white." And sometimes nonlinguistic conditions and linguistic environment work together to make a sentence unambiguous. Of course, it sometimes happens that either or both of these is insufficient, and the sentence remains ambiguous. So a given sentence may or may not be ambiguous depending on the situation in which it occurs. We know how to guard against uttering ambiguous word sequences: we make sure that certain nonlinguistic conditions obtain, or we provide other sentences.

Lacking the appropriate conditions, a sentence on a certain occasion may be ambiguous, but that's just the way things turn out sometimes, even when one tries hard. Suppose I suddenly realize that what I said to you yesterday was ambiguous. I phone you and straighten things out. Still, what I said yesterday, taken by itself, remains ambiguous; what is no longer ambiguous after the phone conversation is what I *meant* (or intended to say) yesterday. With yesterday's conversation plus today's phone conversation, I have now succeeded in saying what I meant to say. When the sentences uttered yesterday and the sentences uttered today are taken as constituting a single disclosure, they mean what I meant all along.

The confusion which underlies the intentionalist's view of ambiguity and intention arises from his failure to distinguish between what an utterance means and what someone meant (or means) by the utterance. I cannot make "I saw her duck" mean that I saw a duck which was a bird *simply* by uttering "I saw her duck" or by uttering "I saw her duck" and *intending* the bird interpretation. An act of intending will get me nowhere. What I have to do is utter "I saw her duck" and then do something else—point my finger, utter other sentences, or the like—or see that certain conditions obtain. Given 1) a discourse, 2) the nonlinguistic conditions under which the discourse was uttered, and 3) a specified language community, a sentence in the discourse will have a specific meaning or remain ambiguous.

But even if one knows what a sentence means in a given discourse, there still may be some doubt as to what the speaker of the discourse meant by the utterance. Suppose that in a certain discourse "I saw her duck" means the speaker saw a woman lower her head. Keeping in mind the distinction between 1) the meaning *of* an utterance and 2) what someone means or meant *by* the utterance, it can be noted that the speaker might have *meant* by the utterance any one or more of a number of things on one or more different levels. On the most basic level, the speaker might have meant (and no doubt did mean, unless he is an inept or unlucky user of English) what he wanted the utterance to mean in that discourse, namely, that he saw a woman lower her head. I call this the most basic level because unless a speaker succeeds in having his utterance mean what he wants it to mean, he cannot usually succeed in doing anything else which he wants to do through his utterance. On another level, the speaker might have meant to impugn a woman's courage, to insult her, to comment on her agility, to praise her, and so on. On still another level, the speaker might have meant to produce certain effects or reactions—to make a woman unhappy or to make her happy. The number of different things a speaker might have meant by an utterance is large, but what a sentence means places limitations on what a person can succeed in meaning by uttering the given sentence. The main point here is that a distinction exists between what a sentence means in a given context and what some speaker may have meant (intended to mean) as he uttered the sentence.

The description of language and meaning given thus far has been developed in terms of "ordinary" situations, but when one turns to literature, the situation is different in certain important respects. What I have to say about literature will also apply in some degree to most written discourse, but I am concerned here only with literature. First, there is a dramatic speaker in the case of literature, so that the typical literary situation is more complicated than the ordinary situation. In an ordinary situation there are simply a speaker and his utterances, but in a literary situation there are the author, the dramatic speaker (or speakers), and the utterances of the dramatic speaker. It is important not to confuse the author *of* a work with a dramatic speaker *in* the work. Shakespeare is the author of the play *Hamlet,* but the character Hamlet is one of the dramatic speakers in the play. In a novel the dramatic speaker is the person who tells the story, for example, Ishmael in *Moby Dick.* Of course, in many novels the dramatic speaker is not named and does not refer to himself. Second, literature is different with regard to the second of the three general conditions mentioned on pages 114–5 for determining the ambiguity or nonambiguity of sentences. The first and third conditions seem to hold for both ordinary and literary situations.

1) *The discourse condition.* In happy cases,we have the complete discourse—a complete conversation, a complete treatise on astronomy, a complete poem, a complete novel. These cases are happy because when we have a complete text, we have all there is to have for determining whether or not a sentence is ambiguous, so far as this condition is concerned. In unhappy cases, we either know the discourse is incomplete or cannot tell whether or not it is complete. These cases are unhappy because, although we can determine whether a given sentence is ambiguous or not relative to the possibly incomplete discourse, we know that our determination of ambiguity might change if we had the complete discourse.

3) *The knowledge-of-a-language condition.* In happy cases, we know the language of some language community—twentieth-century American English, some regional variation of twentieth-century American English, sixteenth-century Elizabethan English, some regional variation of sixteenth-century Elizabethan English, and so on—in terms of which we can understand a discourse and determine whether or not a given sentence is ambiguous. In unhappy cases, we lack to some degree or other knowledge of the language in terms of which we are to understand a discourse.

It must be made clear what is involved in the knowledge-of-a-language condition and what is and is not involved in the inquiry necessary to find out what a word, phrase, or sentence means in a discourse in a certain language. In order to understand a given sentence in a discourse written in sixteenth-century English, I may have to do research into the meaning of a certain word. But in finding out what that word means in sixteenth-century English, I am not inquiring into what the sixteenth-century author of the discourse in question meant by the word. (I am ignoring the differences between the meanings of words and the meanings of sentences here.) The distinction between what a speaker meant by his utterance and what his utterance means is crucial here. It is conceivable that the discovery through, say, some historical record of what an author meant by a word would serve as a clue to what the word means in the language of the author's day. But the distinction I am insisting on still remains: what a particular author meant by a word or an utterance on a particular occasion of its use does not give that word or utterance its meaning in a language. To think otherwise is to get things backwards. The meaning of a word or an utterance in a language comes first, and a particular speaker can then use that meaning on a particular occasion to mean something. The order spoken of here is logical order, not a temporal order.

We now come to the second general condition in which ordinary and literary situations differ: the nonlinguistic conditions under which the discourse is uttered. In ordinary situations, these conditions would be such things as pointing one's finger, the fact that the hearer can see who the speaker is, the fact that a member of the family Anatidae is present, and so on. But in literary situations—for example, with poems and novels—the question of nonlinguistic conditions does not arise, at least does not typically arise. A dramatic speaker in a novel or poem cannot point a finger at a member of the family Anatidae or at a woman present, because although such dramatic speakers can *refer to* things outside the world of the literary work, they cannot *point* to such things. A hearer (a reader) cannot see who the speaker is because dramatic speakers in a novel or poem cannot be seen. A reader can be *told* what such a dramatic speaker looks like even though a dramatic speaker can never be seen, but this is a linguistic matter and not a question of nonlinguistic conditions. The point is that sentences in a literary situation —that is, in poems, novels, and the like—do not typically have nonlinguistic contexts. Consider the contrasting ways in which the same sentence might function in an ordinary situation and a literary one. In an ordinary situation, the utterance of the sentence " 'Twas on yonder hill that the battle was fought" is not ambiguous with regard to the referent of "hill" if only one hill is visible. However, it is ambiguous if two hills are visible and nothing is done to indicate which hill is being referred to. But if " 'Twas on yonder hill that the battle was fought" occurs in a literary work, there cannot be any ambiguity of reference that involves a nonlinguistic context of the utterance. Of course, there may be an ambiguity of reference *within* the story of the work as, for example, when a second character says, "Which of those two hills?" Although there is a reference context established by the utterances which make up a literary work, this kind of context does not exist independently of the discourse and is very different from the context of ordinary situations.

My point is that the nature of literary works is such that they do not typically have nonlinguistic contexts as ordinary discourse does. (Some ordinary situations wholly or partially lack nonlinguistic contexts—for example, phone conversations.) There is nothing necessary about this; it is merely a fact of our *practice*, or way, of literary life. It could have been that all our literary works were such that in order for all the sentences in them to be unambiguous they would have had to be performed in specific geographical locations or replicas of such locations or in geographical locations or replicas of them which possessed certain kinds of features. Of course, some of our literary works do require such settings—namely, plays and movies—and a full discussion of literature would require a detailed treatment of such works. But I am concerned with literary works such as poems and novels which are typically experienced (read) without any nonlinguistic context. Our practice is that these literary works ordinarily do not have nonlinguistic contexts. Consequently, an author of a poem or novel ordinarily must fail or succeed in having dramatic speakers mean that he intends them to mean without depending on the presence of a nonlinguistic context. (I am not suggesting that such failure or success is significant for interpretation.) Attempts to make use of a nonlinguistic context to remove ambiguity are almost always doomed to failure. One possible kind of exception to this might be the case of a novel set in a specfic, well-known geographical location. In this case, the knowledge of the geographical terrain may be thought of as a condition which the dramatic speaker has made sure obtains and which may serve to make some sentence in the discourse unambiguous.

The main point here is that meaning is a *public* matter, not a matter of what an author or, more generally, a speaker intended in the privacy of his mind. So if an author tells us what his poem means but it is not possible to discover that meaning in the poem independently of the author's statement, then it cannot be claimed that the poem means what its author claims it means. The fact that the author had certain intentions in mind when he wrote out the words of his poem does not guarantee that those intentions are embodied in those words. Authors and ordinary speakers alike sometimes fail to say what they mean to say, and although an appeal to intentions can help clear up what was meant by the original words, such an appeal cannot change the meaning (or meaninglessness) of the original words. To forestall one possible misunderstanding it should be made clear that an author may act as a critic to explicate, interpret, and even evaluate his own work, and he may be a good or bad critic. The anti-intentionalist denies that an author has a privileged position as a critic because of his intimate knowledge of his own intention (a critic can only work with the public meaning he finds in the literary work).

Representation in the visual arts is similar to meaning in literature insofar as the artist's intention is concerned. An

artist's intending that his design represent an apple or a
woman or Churchill does not accomplish anything. It is the
properties of the design itself which determine what it represents. True, an artist or anyone else acting as a critic might
call our attention to certain properties of the design which
we have not noticed and enable us to see that the design
represents (or perhaps suggests) a certain object or person.
But this simply means we had failed to take account of what
was publicly there to see and in no way need involve the intentions of the artist.

The interpretation of symbols in painting and literature
is also a public matter. Symbols such as halos have a conventional, public meaning similar to the way in which words
have public meaning. It is true that symbols are sometimes
created or established by a work of art, but this is done in a
public way by having the symbol play a certain role in the
painting or literary work. The meaning of a symbol is not
established by the artist's intention.

The question of correct performance and the intention of
the artist is different from the above because more than
understanding is involved. In addition, two distinct problems
are involved in performance: 1) in a playscript or musical
score, there is always some leeway, for the artist never specifies how each element is to be performed; and 2) in a given
performance, actual stage or score directions may be ignored,
or certain elements (a passage, a scene, an act) may be omitted. The advice of the intentionalist critic to follow the
intention of the artist is vacuous in the first case, because if
there is leeway for the performer, *there is leeway,* and that
is all there is to it.

However, the second case is different. If something is
omitted, then the intention of the artist is knowingly flouted
by the performer (director, composer, arranger, i.e., whoever
has the responsibility for the performance). In this case, the
intentionalist critic feels that violence has been done to the
work of art. It is true that the identity of the work has been
disturbed and perhaps even radically changed. But so what?

If a critic is concerned with the description, interpretation, or evaluation of the performance of a work, what difference does it make that the performance he experiences and talks about is derived by altering an existing work? The critic can still explain and evaluate the performance he has experienced. The critic might say, among other things, that the performance would have been better if something were added at a certain point, and he might or might not be specific about what was missing. If the missing element in a performed work well known to the critic corresponds to some element omitted by a performer, director, etc., then the critic might be very specific and correctly say that the omitted element was just what the performed work needed. On the other hand, in a given case the critic might correctly say that the performed work was better without the element in question.

The point is that the critic must talk about and evaluate the performed work. He may also speculate about why a performed work is good or bad. In some cases, he can correctly say that if the artist's intention had not been flouted, the performed work would be better. But the badness of the performed work would not be due to flouting the artist's intention; it would be due to the *specific change* the director or conductor made. When one undertakes to alter the identity of art, one incurs the dangers inherent in creative work —namely, the danger of creating an inferior thing. However, there is also the possibility of creating something positively good, and this makes the chance worth taking.

From the point of view of the criticism of performed works of art, it is what meets the eye and ear that is described and judged. It is the uncut *Hamlet*, a cut version, a version in modern dress, and so on, which is described and judged, not Shakespeare's intentions. Criticism is concerned with helping us to understand art and to distinguish good art from bad, and the intentions of artists do not have a privileged role to play in the carrying out of either task.

## Chapter 13. Symbolism in Art

SYMBOLS are associated in the minds of some with the occult and magic. The connection is not a necessary one, and there is nothing magical about the way symbols function in art. There is nothing mysterious about the symbolic process, although in given cases the process may be very complicated. There is also nothing inherently valuable about symbolism in art—symbolism is a means of conveying meaning and it can be done well or clumsily. Symbolism can be tastefully and economically employed, but it can be overdone and heavy-handed. Symbolism can enhance a work of art, or it can be a burden.[3]

The symbols which we deal with most frequently are words. The account given of symbols here is, however, not concerned with words but with symbols *in* art. I am concerned here with symbols as they occur in paintings, poems, plays, and so on. Literary works are built up out of symbols (words), but I am concerned with the symbols which result from the description that words provide. In a painting, something, e.g., a lamb, is depicted, and the depicted thing in turn may function as a symbol of something, e.g., of Christ. Similarly, in a literary work something is described, and it is the described thing which may function as a symbol. Symbols in art and words have in common the symbolic function of bearing meaning, and the account of symbolism given here will exhibit this common feature. An account of the symbolic functioning of words, however, would be more complicated than an account of symbolism in art and will not be undertaken here.

Before attempting to formulate a definition of symbolism

in art, it will be helpful to give several examples of such symbolism and describe how they work. Gören Hermerén, drawing on Panofsky, cites the following case of symbolism.[4] In a Jan van Eyck painting, a throne is depicted on the arm-rest of which there is a brass figure of a pelican. The pelican is a traditional Christian symbol for Christ. This is an inter-esting case because the pelican seems like such an unlikely candidate for this particular symbolism. The basis for the symbolism is the belief stated in a bestiary of the twelfth century that the pelican is a devoted parent. According to the bestiary, the young strike their parents with their wings and the parents strike back and kill them. After three days, how-ever, the mother pelican pierces her breast, pouring out her blood over the dead bodies of her young, and this brings them back to life. The attribution to the pelican of the power to revive life serves as the basis for the representation of a pelican to symbolize Christ, to whom similar powers are attributed.

For a present-day example of symbolism, consider Hem-ingway's short story, "A Clean, Well-Lighted Place." In the opening sentence of the story, an old man is described as "an old man who sat in the shadow the leaves of the tree made against the electric light." A dozen or so lines later it is said of him, "the old man sat in the shadow of the leaves of the tree that moved slightly in the wind." A few lines later he is described simply as "the old man sitting in the shadow." The thrice-repeated image of sitting in the shadow is clearly a symbol of approaching death and nothingness.

Isabel Hungerland cites an example of symbolism from the movie *Lost Horizon*.[5] As the High Lama of Shangri-La dies, the camera focuses on a lighted candle being extin-guished by the wind. We know the High Lama has died when the candle goes out because the extinguished candle symbolizes his death.

In the Grünewald Isenheim alterpiece, "The Crucifixion," a lamb stands at the foot of the cross. The lamb carries a small cross on its shoulder held with its right front leg. The lamb with cross is clearly a symbol, presumably for the sacrifice of Christ, which is also the main subject of the painting. The cross itself is a symbol for Christianity, the flag is a symbol of a nation, and the eagle on a United States quarter is a symbol of certain characteristics attributed to the nation, such as strength and nobility. Mrs. Hungerland cites the symbolism involved in number superstitions. She presumably has in mind cases of numbers being symbolic of some state or event.[6] For example, the number seven is symbolic of good luck and the number thirteen of bad luck.

If the foregoing are taken as genuine cases of symbolism, then certain features can be noted about symbolism. 1) A symbol does not, as some assume, have to be concrete, i.e., nonabstract. A number is not concrete and of course words are not concrete either. No doubt most symbols in art are concrete, but in formulating a definition of "symbol" only characteristics uniformly true of symbols can be used. 2) The things which symbols symbolize are quite varied—for example, a person (Christ), an event and a state (death and nothingness), an event (the High Lama's death), an action (Christ's sacrifice), institutions (Christianity and a nation), and qualities (strength and nobility). There seems to be no reason to try to limit the types of things which can be symbolized. 3) In the case of visual art a symbol does not depict what it symbolizes, and in the case of literary art a symbol does not describe what it symbolizes. Symbols convey meaning in a more indirect way than depiction and description, but they build on and enhance depiction and description. 4) A symbol "stands for" in some establishable way that which it symbolizes. A symbol serves to transfer someone's thought to something other than itself, and the transfer is not a random association. The transfer depends upon certain features of the symbol which give it a place in a certain meaning system. 5) None of the symbols cited is a natural sign, such as clouds signifying rain or smoke signifying fire. Natural signs depend on causal relations between sign and thing signified. Natural signs are usually distinguished from symbols, presumably because a symbol achieves the status of being a symbol as the result of some person's action, whereas a natural sign signifies quite independently of anyone's action. In the case of a natural sign, one merely notes causal regularities. However, there is a certain vagueness here and one must be cautious.

Perhaps a definition may now be attempted, but as Mrs. Hungerland notes, the variety of ways that the word "symbol" has been used is so large that probably no definition could cover them all.[7] What has to be done is to focus on a set of examples which one hopes is representative of the bulk of the uses of "symbol" and the members of which one hopes are sufficiently similar to provide a basis for a definition.

> Something is a symbol if and only if for some person or group of persons that thing stands in some establishable way for some other thing and that thing (which is the symbol) does not depict or describe the other thing (that which is symbolized) and the relationship between the thing which signifies and the thing signified is not simply that of a natural sign.

The most important question raised by this definition is that of the *establishment* of the standing-for relation. Perhaps the best way to explain this is to begin by talking about firmly established symbols such as the cross. The cross has for hundreds of years had a central place in Christian ceremonies because of the manner of the martyrdom of Jesus. Such symbols as the cross are a kind of capital for artists to draw upon. The artist can count on all the members of his audience knowing what the cross signifies if he uses it in his work. Such symbols are very much like common words which all members of the community know the meaning of. However, all this talk about the cross or other firmly established symbols does not show how symbols are established, but only that they are established symbols. How, for example, was the cross established as a symbol? One can only speculate about the details of its establishment. At some time, some early Christians must have drawn or fashioned a cross in the presence of other Christians who knew the story of Jesus' martyrdom in order to enhance a ceremony or perhaps to establish his identity as a member of the sect or for some other purpose. In any event, because of the use of a cross in one of the basic events of Christian history, the depicted or fashioned cross became established as a symbol of Christianity. Thus some early Christian by action established the *convention* that the cross is a symbol, and the convention was accepted and used by members of the Christian community. In time the symbolic significance of the cross became known to non-Christians as well.

Conventions may be established in formal and informal ways. Flags as symbols of nations are probably most often established in a formal way. No doubt, at some early moment in the history of the United States, some member of Congress proposed that a flag with thirteen stars and thirteen stripes, etc., be adopted as the flag of the United States, and the proposal was accepted by a majority vote of Congress. However, the establishment of most symbols is informal and consists in some person using something in such a way as to show that it is being used to signify a certain thing.

Artists can employ already established symbols in their work, but just as they create stories, paintings, and plays, artists also create symbols. Artists employ a variety of devices to help establish something as a symbol and no doubt there are some devices as yet not invented, but the following examples will serve to illustrate the ways in which devices are used to help establish new symbols. One way is to depict a very unusual or impossible event in a painting which otherwise depicts an ordinary or historical event. In the Grünewald painting "The Crucifixion," the lamb carrying a little cross on its shoulder supported by holding its leg around the bottom of the cross is a case in point. Even if the lamb were not already an established symbol, this depiction would clearly serve to establish it as a symbol. In some cases when descriptions of unusual or impossible events are given in literary works, they function as symbols.

Another device is to give a depiction or a description a prominent place in the work. The lamb in the Grünewald painting is an example of this device also; it is located in the center foreground of the painting at the foot of the cross. In the Hemingway story, the old man is described as sitting in the shadow in the very first sentence. The end of a work is another prominent place; other prominent places would be relative to the plot or to other formal characteristics. Other devices are repetition and juxtaposition. The description of the old man sitting in the shadow is given three times at the opening of the Hemingway story, and darkness is frequently juxtaposed with light that signifies life and youth. Juxtaposition, whether repeated or not, may serve to establish a symbolic relation. The lamb in the Grünewald painting is shown right next to the crucified Christ, whom it symbolizes.

Such devices alone, however, cannot establish something as a symbol: a thing must have certain appropriate characteristics in order to function as a symbol of a given other thing. Appropriately presented in a work of art, it is relatively easy to make a lamb a symbol of Christ and his sacrifice, for it is believed that lambs have such dominant characteristics as meekness, which is also attributed to Christ, and it is a well-known historical fact that lambs were a traditional sacrifical animal for the Jews. In the case of the old man sitting in the shadow, the easy association of darkness with death and the relation of the phrase to "the valley of the shadow of death" in the Twenty-third Psalm provide a sufficient basis for the described situation to function as a symbol. The basis of a pelican symbolizing Christ is the power attributed to it to revive life. The fact that no one now believes the pelican has this power does not prevent it from functioning as a symbol of Christ. It is not likely, however, that a present-day artist would use a pelican as such a symbol, although he might use a lamb.

In general, it takes both formal devices and a thing with appropriate characteristics to establish that thing or make it function as a symbol. Not every depicted lamb is a symbol of Christ or anything else. A lamb in a painting of Little Bo Peep probably would not symbolize anything. Symbols are context dependent. The way the elements of a work of art work together to enable one element to function as a symbol is well illustrated by the example of the candle and the High Lama. A candle burning and then going out is similar in certain respects to a person being alive and then dying, but these similarities by themselves cannot establish a symbolic relation. The extinguished candle is also similar to a tire which goes flat, but in this instance it is not a symbol of a tire going flat. The extinguished candle is exactly similar to another extinguished candle, but the former is not a symbol of the latter. Similarity is not enough; it is the treatment in the context of the work that picks out the relevant similarities and establishes the symbolic relation. In the movie there is first a shot of the High Lama, who is obviously at the point of death. The camera then cuts to a shot of a candle flickering before an open window. The wind coming through the window blows the candle out. The extinguishing of the candle symbolizes the death of the High Lama because the immediate temporal juxtaposition of the two shots provides the linkage between them and brings out the relevant similarities which establish the symbolic relation. Given another context, the extinguishing of a candle might symbolize a tire going flat.

An artist may try to establish something as a symbol and fail, because he does not put the elements of his work together properly or because he does not provide certain crucial elements. If the film editor of *Lost Horizon* had mistakenly placed the candle shot far removed from the death scene, then it would not have functioned as a symbol of the High Lama's death, although it would still have the aura of being a symbol. It is also possible and probably frequently occurs that artists place things in their works which have the aura of being symbols but which in fact do not succeed in being symbols. Masses of such "symbols" in a work of art would lend to it the appearance of significance. Perhaps some of the strange things in surrealist art are this kind of symbol. Beardsley says that Kafka's "In the Penal Colony" has the "air of being deeply and richly symbolic, without symbolizing anything in particular, or at least anything that you can formulate in other words."[8]

But what is the point of symbols in art? What function do they serve? Most fundamentally, symbols in art convey meaning or information. The image of sitting in the shadow conveys the meaning "is near death." The depicted lamb with cross on its shoulder conveys the meaning "the crucified Christ." The extinguished candle conveys the information "the High Lama is dead." In some cases the meaning conveyed might be grammatically best formulated as a statement (the candle), in other cases as an adjectival phrase (the lamb with cross), in still other cases as a predicate (the shadow), and in still other cases in other ways. The point is that in one form or other meaning is conveyed.

The information conveyed may be additional information or it may be redundant. In the case of the extinguished candle, additional information is conveyed—when the candle goes out we know for the first time that the High Lama is dead. The lamb with the cross bears redundant meaning, for the central focus of the painting is the depiction of the crucified Christ. One would probably want to say that the meaning conveyed by the image of sitting in shadow is also redundant because the old man's situation is made abundantly clear by the straight-forward nonsymbolic aspects of the story. It is probably the case that the large majority of symbols are redundant and most symbols could be dispensed with without any loss of meaning. One could, for example, simply show the High Lama dying or say the old man feels the nearness of death.

But this technical kind of redundancy is not a defect in art, nor even in ordinary speech. The redundancy of ordinary speech ensures that what we say is understood. The redundant meaning of symbols adds a thickness and richness of texture to a work of art. Symbols can at once add to the complexity and maintain or increase the unity of a work of art. Consider the Grünewald painting without the lamb with cross. Then add the lamb to the painting. With the lamb the painting is more complex than without the lamb because it has more elements. The lamb maintains or perhaps increases the unity of the painting because the symbolic meaning of the lamb fits in with the other elements and the main theme of the painting. Of course, not every symbol will enhance a work of art: a given symbol might tend to make a given work incoherent, and too many symbols, even if coherent, may spoil a work.

Symbols typically serve to emphasize and reinforce the main theme or themes of a work. In some cases, symbols properly used give a work a brooding intensity similar to that given by repeated chant. The kind of effect given by symbols could not have been achieved by simple repetition in the basic mode of expression (depiction or description). Such repetition would be boring or even silly: imagine replacing the lamb with cross at the foot of the cross with a small depiction of the crucifixion. Also in some instances, the symbol further serves to emphasize certain specific features of what is symbolized—in the instance of the lamb with the cross, the meekness of Jesus and the sacrificial nature of the event. Symbols work in subtle and complicated ways.

The impact of symbols is not simply the result of the fact that they convey meaning in a manner different from depiction or description; the economy with which they function is important too. A symbol may not, like the proverbial picture, be worth ten thousand words, but it may be worth many words or much depiction. A symbol packs a great deal of information into a small compass. And an established symbol serves to sum up a lot of significant history and experience—it is a repository of meaning.

There is at least one sort of thing for which the word "symbol" is used that might be expressed better in a different way. For example, it is sometimes said that Willie Loman in *Death of a Salesman* is a symbol of a certain kind of man or a certain kind of life. To say that Willie Loman is a symbol means that the character and his actions *stand for* a certain kind of man or life and *transfer* our thought to that kind of man or life. Putting the matter in these terms, however, fails to do justice to the experience of this play. Willie Loman does not stand for a certain kind of man or life; he is a fictional *example* of that kind of man or life. Willie Loman is an illustration or exemplification rather than a symbol. An example is more powerful and direct and less subtle than a symbol. Both exemplification and symbolization serve to call our attention to certain kinds of things and each has its place in art. However, there is not, I think, any good reason for calling exemplification a kind of symbolization.

## Chapter 14. Metaphor

METAPHOR has probably attracted more critical attention than any other figure of speech. This attention is partly a function of the great frequency with which metaphors occur in poetry. If poetic language is to be understood, an account of metaphor must be given. Metaphors also occur in prose, and not just in "literary" prose. Metaphors are used by sportswriters, scientists, philosophers, businessmen, and housewives. And they are as much a feature of speech as of written language. Metaphor is a pervasive and powerful aspect of language. It is, therefore, highly desirable to have an account of how metaphors function, or to have what is sometimes called a "theory of metaphor."[9]

The word "metaphor" is sometimes used in a very broad sense, but it is being used here to refer to certain kinds of sentences and phrases within sentences. The following is a list of sample metaphors:

1. The chairman ploughed through the discussion.
2. A smokescreen of witnesses.
3. Light is but the shadow of God.[10]
4. The smoke is briars.[11]

Note that certain words in these phrases and sentences— "ploughed" and "smokescreen," for example—stand out as metaphorical and contrast with the other words in the expressions.

In order to understand metaphor, it will be helpful first

to discuss another figure of speech—simile. Discussion of this figure will provide a background and an opportunity to develop some terminology with which to analyze metaphor. A simile, according to the traditional account, means literally what it says and explicitly compares one thing with another. For example, "The boy runs like a deer" is a simile which asserts of a certain boy that certain features of his running resembles the running of a deer. Of course, not every feature of a deer's running is being predicated of the boy's running—for example, running on four legs. This example is an *open* simile in that the hearer must figure out from the context—the other words in the sentence and the other sentences in the discourse of which the sentence is a part—which features of a deer's running are being attributed to the boy. A *closed* simile specifies the respect or respects in which the two things compared are alike. The open-simile example can be closed by adding a few words—"The boy runs like a deer with respect to grace" or, more idiomatically, "The boy runs as gracefully as a deer."

Similes are, then, literal. What is meant by "literal"? A word is used literally when it is used in one of its dictionary senses. The literal meaning of a sentence is the meaning it has as a function of the literal meanings of the words in it. A basic question about metaphor can now be asked: is metaphor a species of literal language like simile?

The oldest and most widely held view, one which can be traced back to Aristotle, is that a metaphor is a *disguised* simile which makes an implied comparison. Several other theories of metaphor have been advanced, but they lack the plausibility and influence of the disguised-simile theory and will not be discussed here.[12] According to the disguised-simile view, a metaphor has meaning in a literal, although somewhat roundabout, way. Max Black calls this theory "the comparison view"[13] and Beardsley calls it "the object-comparison view."[14] The reason for using the word "object" is to bring out that the theory maintains that a metaphorical word literally refers to an object or process which is then compared by the hearer to the object or process referred to by the nonmetaphorical words. Consider the detailed account that the object-comparison view would give of the metaphor embedded in the sentence "the defense attorney presented a smokescreen of witnesses." A hearer would understand the word "witnesses" to refer to certain witnesses (objects) and the word "smokescreen" to refer to a smokescreen. The hearer would then compare the two referents and work out what is being said by means of a comparison. The object-comparison theory claims that the way metaphorical words mean depends on both of two aspects of words. First, words have *senses,* or meanings which are specified in terms of other words. The sense of a word is given in a dictionary. Second, some words and expressions *refer* or purport to refer to objects or processes. A sense of the word "cat" is "a carnivorous mammal (Felis catus) . . . etc." The referent of "cat" in "The cat is on the mat" is a nonlinguistic object, namely, a particular cat.

The problem with the object-comparison view is that although, for example, the referent of "witnesses" is clear enough—it is the group of witnesses presented by the defense attorney—the referent of the metaphorical word "smokescreen" is a mystery. Which smokescreen is being referred to in order that a comparison can be made? Clearly no particular smokescreen is being referred to as is the case in the sentence "Remember the smokescreen that was laid down before we went into Omaha Beach." In this sentence "the smokescreen . . ." functions as a referring expression and purports to refer to a particular smokescreen (object). The word "smokescreen" in the metaphorical expression does not refer; it functions like, say, "large number" in "a large number of witnesses," namely, to modify the word "witnesses." In short, the complete function of "smokescreen" *in the metaphorical expression* is carried out simply in terms of the sense of "smokescreen" without referring. In the literal sentence "John is a student," the proper name "John" refers to some particular person (object), but "a student" does not refer to anything; it simply applies a sense of the word to the subject of the sentence. Of course, in some sentences "a student" may have a referring function—for example, in "A student left a package." When a word is used in a sentence or a phrase, its sense is always used, but a word does not refer unless it is used to do so. In "Monkeys are mammals," the word "monkeys" refers to the *class* of monkeys, and something is said about each member of the class referred to. In "Jocko and George are monkeys," the sense of "monkeys" is used, but "monkeys" does not refer to anything. "Jocko" and "George" refer to two individuals, who incidentally happen to be monkeys. In the metaphorical sentence (about a human being), "John is a sheep," the metaphorical expression "a sheep" functions just as "a student" does in the first literal sentence and as "monkeys" does in "Jocko and George are monkeys." That is, "a sheep" applies a sense (metaphorical in this case) to a subject of a sentence and has no referring function.

The main point of these remarks is that even in those cases in which it might be thought that the object-comparison account might work best—namely, cases in which the metaphorical expression is a noun or a noun phrase—it does not work. Even in these cases, the metaphorical word does not refer and hence does not designate a referent to which something can be compared. In a sentence such as "My uncle is like your uncle" both "My uncle" and "your uncle" refer and designate two objects which can be compared, and we may say that the sentence is a comparison. It should be clear by now that metaphors are not comparisons. Beardsley presents an argument against the object-comparison view which fits in nicely with the above. He considers T. S. Eliot's line from "East Coker":

> frigid purgatorical fires
> of which the flame is roses, and the smoke is briars.[15]

In the metaphor "the smoke is briars" the object-comparison view would be that "briars" refers to briars and that we get the meaning of the metaphor by comparing the smoke and its properties with briars and their properties in order to understand what is being said about the smoke. However, an important part of the meaning of "briars" in this case comes from the way the crown of thorns figures in the Bible story of the crucifixion. It is impossible to work out the meaning derived from the Biblical association by reflecting on briars and their properties—their scratchiness, and so on. The word "briars" has acquired a nonliteral meaning as a result of an historical event, and such meaning can be exploited by the poet. Such meaning is not idiosyncratic or private to the poet; it derives from a well-known event and is public. Mythological stories are as good as historical events for providing the foundation for this kind of meaning. Note that this argument shifts the emphasis away from objects and their properties to words and their meanings.

The object-comparison theory is not only mistaken about reference, it is more complicated than it needs to be. In the comparison view, a metaphor operates in two stages: in the first stage the metaphorical word, say, "smokescreen" *by virtue of its meaning* refers to an object; in the second stage the object referred to is compared to some other object. In the view advanced by Beardsley as correct, which he calls "the verbal-opposition theory," it is maintained that metaphorical words function completely on the level of the first stage without referring to an object.

According to the verbal-opposition view,[16] words have their primary, or dictionary, meanings, and when these senses are used, literal expressions result. In addition to these primary meanings, words have other meanings. Some of these secondary meanings are the result of what Max Black calls "systems of associated commonplaces."[17] Some of the associated commonplaces are associations such as briars with Jesus' crown of thorns, and some involve characteristics commonly (truly or falsely) attributed to some thing. For example, it is commonly believed that wolverines are fierce. Such meanings are common capital from which metaphors can be constructed. Other secondary senses are generated by the metaphors and the contexts in which they occur. For example, the metaphorical meaning of "smokescreen" in "a smokescreen of witnesses" is generated by an abstraction of the dictionary meaning of "smokescreen" from "a curtain of heavy smoke, often produced by chemicals, used as a concealing screen, as for naval vessels" to something less specific like "a device for concealing something." In addition to abstraction, there are many ways in which secondary meanings are generated, but the significant point is that (some) words have meanings other than their dictionary meanings.

How are secondary senses activated to mean what they mean in a particular metaphor? Beardsley speaks of a logical opposition between the literal words and the metaphorical word which rules out a literal interpretation of the meaning of the metaphorical word and shows that the word must be understood in a nonliteral way. I am not sure if logical *opposition* is the best way to put it, but he is probably on the right track. In any case, what goes on in understanding a word metaphorically is basically the same as what goes on in understanding a word literally. A given word may, for example, have three distinct literal meanings, each sense being numbered in the dictionary. However, when this word is used literally in a sentence, it is not numbered to indicate which of the literal senses it means. We have to figure out which literal sense fits the sentence and its context. If this cannot be done, the sentence is ambiguous or obscure. The same kind of sorting process is involved when a word is used metaphorically in an expression: each one of the literal meanings is in one way or another ruled out, and in the search for the meaning that fits we must go on to the "list" of nonliteral senses that the word may already have. If the nonliteral "list" fails us, we go on to try to find what new meaning is created by the metaphor and its context. Of course, I do not mean to suggest that we go through the process in such a mechanical way; I am just specifying the elements that are involved in the process.

Let me examine the kind of process that we go through in understanding the metaphorical sentence "The chairman ploughed through the discussion." A metaphorical sentence typically contains substantive words (nouns, verbs, adjectives) which are literal and substantive words which are metaphorical, as does this example. However, which words are metaphorical and which literal cannot be known *until the whole sentence is understood*. Assume that we read through a sentence one word at a time, absorbing the information in each word as we come to it. I realize that we normally absorb larger chunks at a time than this, but we do go through a written sentence from left to right absorbing the information contained in chunks of some size or other. As we go through a sentence, at various points certain options are opened up to us and certain options are closed off, although what appeared to be closed options at an earlier point may be opened up by information that comes further along in the sentence. When we come to "The" in our sample sentence, several options are opened. For example, it and the words which immediately follow it may constitute a definite description such as "the man on the corner" or an expression referring to a class of individuals such as "the whale (is a mammal)." The occurence of "The" closes off or makes improbable certain options. When we come to "chairman," the two options mentioned still remain. "The chairman" may be a definite description (or part of one) which refers to a person who presides at a meeting or who holds a certain kind of administrative job, or it may refer to the class of chairmen as in the sentence "The chairman is the main administrative officer in an academic department." When we come to "ploughed," it seems most probable that "The chairman" is a definite description, but the second possibility is not entirely ruled out. "Ploughed" is the metaphorical word in the sentence. However, we are not yet in a position to say that it is. There is nothing about being a chairman which rules out ploughing a furrow in the earth or ploughing through the sea (say, with the chairman being pulled through the water, by a rope) or any other of the literal meanings of "ploughed." The word "through" seems to rule out ploughing a field for cultivation, for we would say "ploughed the field" for that, but ploughing through water, a watermain, an oil pipeline, an electrical cable, and so on, remain as possibilities. When we come to "the" and "discussion" everything (or almost everything) falls into place, and we understand the sentence, see that it is a metaphorical sentence, and see that "ploughed" is a metaphorical word in this context. None of the literal senses of "to plough," with one possible exception, fits in such a way as to make the sentence make sense as a literal sentence. The one dictionary sense which is not ruled out by the other words in the sentence is "to proceed laboriously." To take care of this possibility, assume a context for the sentence which rules out this literal sense and requires that the sentence be understood metaphorically to indicate that the chairman dealt ruthlessly and the like with the matters considered in the discussion he chaired.

How do we know to read "ploughed" metaphorically and not some other word or words? There is no general answer to this question. One just has to see what options for understanding are available, given the words in a particular sentence. And of course it is not simply the words in the sentence in question that may be important. The context of the sentence—the spoken or written sentences connected with the sentence in question, the tone of voice or gesture with which the sentence is uttered if it is a spoken sentence, and so on—is frequently crucial. Earlier I gave "John is a sheep" as an example of a metaphor, but there are contexts in which it would be a literal sentence. For example, if someone said, "I have three pet animals: a pig named Jack, a cat named Tom, and one named John who is covered with wool. John is a sheep." In this context it is clear that a literal sense of "sheep" applies.

Sentences such as "John is a sheep" and "Richard is a lion," which are often cited as examples of metaphors, are not really metaphors at all—they are at best "dead metaphors." For example, one of the senses of "lion" given in the dictionary is "a person felt to resemble a lion especially in courage, ferocity, dignity." "Sheep," "bear," "cat," and the like have similar senses specified in the dictionary. Thus to say of some human being that he is a lion is to assert literally that the person is courageous, ferocious, or dignified. (Given the presence of the locution "felt to resemble" in some of these senses, one might be tempted to say that some dead metaphors are similes. But perhaps a better way to conceive of them is to say that dictionaries have been influenced by the object-comparison theory of metaphor in stating some of the senses which produce dead metaphors.) Presumably at some time in the past, "lion" did not have this sense as a literal meaning, and at that time "Richard is a lion" could have been a metaphor. A problem arises about dating the time at which a particular sense became literal. Dictionaries, which I used initially in specifying when a sense is literal or not, are of fairly recent origin, and "lion," "sheep," and so on, must have been used in the way they are currently used for centuries. So although we cannot date the death of "Richard is a lion" as a metaphor, it must have been a very long time ago. Metaphors are born, age in direct proportion to their popularity, and finally reach the dictionary— the graveyard of forgotten metaphors. There is a conceptual problem here too, because the distinction between literal and nonliteral senses of words ultimately depends on actual usage, which is only reflected by dictionaries and reflected always with a time lag. Still, the use of dictionaries is the only practical way for determining the literal senses of words.

I have just said that "Richard is a lion" is a dead metaphor, and as a sentence which asserts that the person named by "Richard" is courageous, etc., it *is* a dead metaphor. It is, however, always possible to revive the sentence as a metaphor, although it will not be an assertion about courage. For example, given a certain context, "Richard is a lion" might be used to say that someone named Richard has a large amount of flowing, tawny-colored hair. The raising of dead metaphors points up the importance of context in understanding the meaning of sentences—metaphorical or literal.

At the beginning of this section a traditional account of simile was given. This account maintains that words are used literally in similes. The question was then posed, "Are metaphors literal like similes?" It is now clear that metaphors are nonliteral; that is, metaphorical sentences and phrases depend on the nonliteral functioning of some word or words in them. Metaphor differs from simile, at least as simile is usually understood.

Reflection on the theory of metaphor advanced here suggests to me that perhaps the traditional view of simile as a comparison is wrong too. Perhaps "like a deer" in "The boy runs like a deer" and "like a red, red rose . . ." in "O my Luve's like a red, red rose . . ." do not refer and hence do not designate an object for comparison. However, this question will not be pursued here, and the reader will have to follow it up on his own.

---

## Chapter 15. Expression

---

IT WAS ARGUED in Chapter 3 that the nineteenth-century theories of art as the expression of emotion are inadequate, and in Chapter 9 an examination of Collingwood's version of the emotional-expression theory yielded the same result. It seems reasonable to suppose that any theory which claims a *necessary* connection between art and the expression of emotion will fail. There have been other kinds of expression theories—art as the expression of wishes, as the expression of unconscious desires, and so on—but these theories have not been nearly as popular as the emotion version. These other theories fail for reasons similar to those cited in regard to the emotion version.

However, even if art cannot be defined in terms of the expression of emotion, it is certainly true that in some sense art frequently expresses emotion. It is an important problem in aesthetics to work out in what sense or senses emotion is expressed by art. Consider first two examples of the account usually given of the expression of emotion in ordinary situations outside of art. A person's beaming face expresses joy. In this situation it is typically assumed that two basic elements are involved: 1) the face with a particular expression on it and 2) the emotion the person is feeling. A person's bitter remark expresses his anger (or some other emotion depending on the context). Again it is typically assumed that two basic elements are involved: 1) the bitter remark and 2) the emotion the person is feeling. In each of these examples there is something public—the face and the remark—and something private, or not observed by spectators or auditors— the felt emotion. It is quite natural to take this picture of ordinary situations as the model for explaining what it means to say that art expresses emotion. When this is done, one is led to look in the artistic situation for something public which is the vehicle of expression and for something private which is expressed by this vehicle. It should be noted that the nonart cases cited are cases in which there are actual emotions felt and a person behaves in such a way as to express his emotion. It is quite possible for someone to behave in an expressive way without any felt emotion, as in acting.

There are three basic items in the artistic situation: 1) the artist, 2) the art he creates, and 3) the audience which experiences the work. Works of art are, of course, public, and it is natural to assume therefore that they are public vehicles for expression. The artist and his audience offer private locations for felt emotions which may stand in relation to works of art. Thus, given the typical assumptions about expressing, two possibilities are immediately suggested: 1) art expresses the emotion of the artist, and 2) art expresses (evokes) emotion in the audience.[18] If a case cannot be made for one of these two theses, the notion that a privately felt emotion is involved when art expresses emotion will have to be given up. In order to avoid certain complications (to be discussed later) introduced by arts in which representation typically occurs, the two possible theses will be discussed as they apply to music. I shall develop my argument by talking about the expression of sadness or joy, assuming them to be typical emotions.

First, consider the possibility that when we say that a particular musical passage expresses joy or sadness, we mean that the music expresses the joy or the sadness of its creator. Call this possibility the "artist thesis." It might at first appear that the kinds of argument used against intentionalist criticism could also be brought to bear against the artist thesis —namely, that to refer to the artist's emotion is to talk about something which is distinct from the work of art. Such an argument would be relevant from the point of view of the philosophy of criticism, which is concerned with aesthetic objects. However, the question must be treated in the wider context of the philosophy of art, and from this point of view, it might conceivably be true that art which expresses joy or sadness does in fact express the joy or sadness of its creator. There are, nevertheless, good reasons to think that the artist thesis is false. In arguing against the artist thesis, it should be admitted at the outset that a given piece of sad music might have been composed during a time when its composer was sad and that his sadness was in part responsible for the sadness in the music. In such a case, it would be reasonable to say that the music served to express the sadness of the composer. However, the artist thesis demands a great deal more than this. It demands that all music expressing sadness be written by a composer in a sad frame of mind, all music expressing joy be written by a composer when he is happy, and so on.

The first difficulty the artist thesis meets is a practical one, namely, the impossible task of empirically confirming that all music expressive of sadness has been or will be written by composers when they are sad. There are little or no data available about the state of mind of composers at the time they compose. So we certainly cannot *know* that the artist thesis is true. The second difficulty the artist thesis must meet is that there is no compelling reason to think that sad music must be written by a person feeling sad. Given a musical passage which all agree expresses sadness, there is no reason to think a person had to be sad in order to write down that particular sequence of notes. It is very easy to imagine a composer in a happy frame of mind being given the commission to write a piece of music which expresses sadness for some sad occasion. Such a composer, if he is competent, ought to be able to do the job required. It must certainly be the case that the artist thesis is false. Thus, although on an occasion when we know that a composer feeling sad composed a sad piece of music we could use the locution "the music expresses sadness" to convey the information that the music expressed the composer's emotion, this cannot be what we generally mean when we say that a particular musical passage expresses sadness.

Consider now what may be called "the audience thesis," namely, the possibility that when we say that a musical passage expresses sadness, we mean that the music evokes the emotion of sadness in the members of the audience that hear the music. The audience thesis would have to meet some rather complicated and sophisticated objections concerning the problem of how a specific emotion such as sadness may be aroused by something as unspecific as music. Some simpler arguments, however, show that this thesis is false. Music which expresses sadness *may* evoke sadness in a hearer, and this seems to occur with some frequency. However, music expressive of sadness certainly does not *always* evoke sadness; for example, a person might listen to a piece of music which expresses sadness, agree that it expresses sadness, and simply be too happy at the moment to feel sad. This particular argument becomes clearer when music expressive of gaiety is considered: a person in a sad frame of mind can seldom have gay feelings evoked by music which expresses gaiety. In fact, such music may make a sad person even sadder. Even if one were to specify that the relevant emotions are evoked by the music in a person in a normal frame of mind (assuming that normal could be adequately characterized in this context), it does not seem plausible that such a person would always be made sad or happy or whatever. Thus we might, on a given occasion, use the locution "the music expresses sadness" to convey the information that a piece of music evokes sadness in a certain individual. However, this is not what we generally mean when we say that a particular musical passage expresses sadness.

If the artist and audience theses are false, there is no private location for felt emotions in connection with music expressing emotion. Consequently, the explanation of how music can express emotion must be given in terms of public phenomena, and the explanation must not contain reference to any felt emotion, that is to say, to any particular actual emotion. The sadness expressed by music does not have the "depth" that the sadness expressed by a sad face has when the sad face is genuine and there is a sad feeling "behind" it. This lack of depth means that the sadness of music does not stand in relation to any particular instance of sad feeling. It is perhaps also worth noting that whereas one can be deceived by a "put-on" sad face into thinking that there are sad feelings behind it, one cannot be deceived in the same way by sad music, for there is nothing behind the music which necessarily stands in relation to its sadness.

If sad music does not necessarily stand in relation to some particular instance of sad feelings then it is unnecessary and misleading to use the verb "expresses" when we want to say what we generally mean when we use the locution "the music expresses sadness." It is misleading because "express" is a relation verb, and its use in this case strongly suggests that there is a relation between the music and some other particular thing. Consequently, the word "express" should be avoided in favor of locutions such as "the music is sad" or "the music has a sad quality." This way of speaking makes it clear that a quality of the music itself is being referred to. Even this kind of usage is not without a minor inconvenience: it might mislead someone who does not realize that the statement is metaphorical into thinking that it is being asserted that some music is actually sad. But what we are doing when we say that the music is sad is to call attention to a certain quality of the music by way of a metaphorical attribution. As we saw in the last chapter, there is nothing wrong with metaphor; in fact, it is a very useful and powerful aspect of language. Frequently when we say music is sad, gay, and so on, we are referring to qualities of music for which we have no literal words.

The avoidance of "express" in favor of "is" or "has" also has the advantage of bringing about a certain theoretical simplicity. Words such as "majestic," "delicate," "vigorous," and "sprightly"—words which do not refer to emotional states or emotions—are used to describe music by means of "is" or "has." We say that music is majestic or vigorous or sprightly or the like. Emotion words like "sad" or "gay" and nonemotion words like "delicate" or "sprightly" may now be handled in the same way. As long as "express" is used in connection with emotion words, the impression is given that emotion words function differently from nonemotion words. It turns out, however, that emotion words and nonemotion words (of the general type mentioned) are both instances of metaphorical description when applied to qualities of music.

Having reached the conclusion that descriptions of qualities of music are cases of metaphorical attribution, this conclusion should be reviewed in the light of some of the results of the preceding chapter on metaphor. From the point of view of usage, it may well be the case that a number of the kind of words discussed in this section have developed literal senses which apply to music. "Sad" and "gay," for example, have been applied with such great frequency to music that we no longer have the feeling of metaphor when they are so used. We may not find these literal senses listed in dictionaries yet—there is always a certain time lag. Although it is a difficult matter to decide, "sad" and "gay" seem to apply as literally to music as "allegro," "has a fast tempo," and so on. Whether the words under discussion all apply to music metaphorically or whether some apply literally and some metaphorically is not really the most important point. The main conclusion of the foregoing argument is that these words describe characteristics of music rather than characteristics of the composer or audience.

The qualities of music referred to by such terms as "sad" probably cannot be characterized in a general way. That is, it may very well be the case, for example, that all pieces of sad music do not have a common feature. Probably most sad music is rather slow-paced, but there might be sad music which is not. And, of course, not all slow music is sad—a certain slow-paced piece might be majestic or stately or even be without any definite character. Still, with certain pieces of music, "sad" will be the best term available for referring to a particular quality of the music; "majestic" will be the best term available for other pieces; and so on.

Music is not the only art with qualities which can be usefully referred to by such terms as "sad" and "gay." For example, people frequently speak of nonrepresentational paintings as sad, gay, lively, delicate, and the like. And, of course, areas in a representational painting may be similarly described; for example, someone might aptly speak of the color of a represented piece of clothing as being painted with a delicate shade of blue or with a gay combination of red and yellow. Similar cases to these can be found in the other arts.

The problem treated in this chapter has been discussed entirely in terms of nonrepresentational aspects of the arts: musical passages, nonrepresentational paintings, and colors in representational painting. Of course, color in a painting may be representational, but the kind of descriptions under discussion do not relate to the representational function of color, only to its various qualities. The reason for restricting the discussion to nonrepresentational aspects is that representation raises complications: is a sad face in a painting sad in the same way that sad music is sad? A depicted face *expresses* sadness in the same way that a real face *expresses* sadness, whereas music is best described as *being* sad. The sad face in a painting is depicted as standing in relation to the sad feelings of the depicted person, whereas sad music does not stand in relation to any particular sad feelings, actual or depicted. There are, of course, problems of explaining what "depicted feelings" means and how such "feelings" could stand in relation to something else, but these problems are too time-consuming to be discussed here.

# PART V

## The Evaluation of Art

### Chapter 16.  Introduction: Beardsley's Theory

THE EVALUATION of art is probably the area in aesthetics in which there is the most widespread disagreement. Consequently, one must be wary and tentative in discussing it. In the previous chapters I have not hesitated to advance theses of my own and argue for them, as well as try to present a variety of basic theories of aesthetics and art. In this final part, my goals will be more limited, and I shall try simply to outline the major evaluational theories which have been developed by philosophers. I shall begin by making a fairly detailed statement of Monroe Beardsley's theory of evaluation[1] and then go on to discuss other theories by contrasting them with and comparing them to Beardsley's theory.

For a number of reasons a consideration of Beardsley's theory is a good introduction to the subject. His account is developed clearly and rather completely and thus serves well to define the area. Beardsley's theory is more complicated than most and therefore has the didactic virtue of displaying many of the features that other theories of evaluation possess. The theory differs in a striking way from most other theories in its analysis of the basic notion of "aesthetic goodness," and this provides an illuminating contrast with other theories. Finally, the theory makes a genuine attempt to take account of the actual practice of critics, something which other philosophers have often failed to do.

When a critic evaluates a work of art, he does not simply say that it is good or bad; he generally gives reasons to back up his evaluation. Sometimes the reasons offered support the value judgment and sometimes they fail to do so. The important point at this juncture is that value judgments can be supported by reasons, although the nature of the support relation may not be clear to us. The central concern of Beardsley's theory is to explore the nature of the support relation, i.e., to show how value judgments can be logically derived from reason statements. The word "good" will be used throughout Chapters 16 and 17 as the value term for which the philosophers under consideration will give an account. The value vocabulary of critics is much richer and contains a host of terms such as "magnificent," "exquisite," "beautiful," and the like. At the end of this chapter, I shall indicate the kind of analysis which might be given for such terms.

Beardsley's theory of evaluation consists of two related parts: 1) an account of critical reasoning about the arts which he calls "the general criterion theory," and 2) an account of the nature of aesthetic value which he calls "the instrumentalist theory of aesthetic value." The latter supports or forms the foundation of the former, although it is possible that the general criterion theory might be justified in some other way.

The distinctive feature of the general criterion theory is the contention that critical reasoning about the arts presupposes general principles upon which judgments about particular works of art *deductively* depend.[2] Examples—although inadequate ones—of general critical principles are "Unified works of art are always good" and "All sad works are good." If these principles were adequate, we would be justified in concluding of any sad work, "This work is good." The necessity of general principles has been vigorously debated in recent philosophical literature. For example, it has been correctly pointed out that certain features are merits in one work of art, but are not merits in other works of art (sometimes they are even defects) . Consequently, it has been argued that there are no general principles involving such features. The argument is that if feature $X$ is sometimes a merit and sometimes not, then a general principle "$X$ is always a merit" cannot be true.

Beardsley's answer to this argument is that there does not have to be a general principle for *every* feature which can be correctly cited as a merit. First, it is frequently misleading to speak of single features in isolation from other features. Feature $A$ may be a merit in a work of art when the work also possesses features $B$ and $C$. However, feature $A$ may not be a merit when the work lacks $B$ and $C$ and possesses features $M$ and $N$. Features frequently work together in clusters, and some features will work together while others will not. Thus, in understanding why a single feature helps make a work of art good, one must frequently see how that feature combines with others. In Beardsley's view, there does not have to be a general principle for every feature which can be correctly cited as a merit. Second, in addition to the working together of features, he also argues that some features are secondary to other features and that only primary features generate general principles. He writes, "For example, suppose the touch of humor (the gravedigger's gags, the drunken porter at the gate) is a merit in one context because it heightens the dramatic tension, but a defect in another context, where it lets the tension down."[3] Clearly a touch of humor is not a *general* merit, but notice that in the cases cited it is a merit because it increases dramatic tension, and in the supposed case in which it lets down dramatic tension it is a defect. Perhaps dramatic tension is always a merit, at least in dramas. Dramatic tension is an instance of *intensity*, which is one of Beardsley's primary criteria. The other two are *unity* and *complexity*. He argues, but he does not pretend to have shown conclusively, that any reason which can correctly be cited as a merit can be subsumed under either unity, intensity, or complexity. Only the presence of unity *or* intensity *or* complexity *always* makes for goodness in a work of art.

Beardsley formulates his definition of primary criteria in the following way:

> Let us say that the properties A, B, C, are the *primary (positive)*
> *criteria* of aesthetic value if the addition of any one of them or
> an increase in it, without a decrease in any of the others, will
> always make the work a better one.[4]

According to this view, a work of art X, which is complex,
unified, and intense, has some good in it. Each of the criteria
is a property which can vary by degrees: one work may be
more unified than another, and so on. Consequently, a work
Y which is quite complex, highly unified, and very intense
would be better than work X. It is worth noting that in certain cases one primary feature may conflict with another.
For example, the particular complexity a given work has may
be of such a kind or degree that the work cannot be very
highly unified; even so, the work may still be very good because it possesses some of the primary features to a high degree. The point is that in particular instances, some primary
feature may not be achievable without sacrificing some other
primary feature.

Beardsley formulates his definition of secondary criteria
in the following way:

> . . . let us say that a given property X is a *secondary (positive)*
> *criterion* of aesthetic value if there is a certain set of other
> properties such that, whenever they are present, the addition
> of X or any increase in it will always produce an increase in
> one or more of the primary criteria.[5]

From what has already been said, it is clear that the secondary features are subordinate to the primary and that their
value to a work is conditional on the presence of other secondary features.

The following simplified dialogue will serve as an example
of the structure of critical reasoning. It is simplified because
only one primary feature is involved. A complete case would
involve a detailed discussion of each of the primary features
and would be much richer in details cited and described.

CRITIC: Cézanne's "The Sainte Victoire, Seen from the
Quarry Called Bibemus" is a good painting.

QUESTIONER: Why?

CRITIC: Because its colors are harmonious and its spatial design of planes and volumes is tightly organized.[6]

QUESTIONER: True, but why does that make the painting good?

CRITIC: Because each of these two is an instance of unity and unity in a work of art is always a good thing.

With his last remark, the critic has arrived at a level basic for critical reasoning, but this remark is still subject to challenge. (Beardsley's answer to such a challenge involves the second part of his theory of evaluation which will be discussed later.) The critic's remarks can be reorganized to show the deductive nature of his reasoning.

| | |
|---|---|
| 1. A unified work always has some good in it. | Assumed premise |
| 2. This painting's colors are harmonious and its spatial design of planes and volumes is tightly organized. | By observation |
| 3. This painting is unified. | From 2 (or by observation) |
| 4. This painting has some good in it. | From 1 and 3 |

It is clear that the deductive reformulation of the critic's remarks does not say as much as the original remarks. Originally it was concluded that the painting is a good painting, but in the reformulation it is concluded only that the painting has some good in it, which is a much weaker conclusion. The original remarks as stated, however, are not deductively valid. To make them valid would require introducing considerations of the degree of unity there is in the painting and of the complexity and intensity of the painting. In short, as a general rule, more than one of the primary criteria are always involved in making a work of art good. A premise such as "A very highly unified work is always good," from which it could be deduced that a highly unified painting *is good*, cannot be used because such a premise is false as a generalization. That it is false can be seen, for example, from the fact that a black dot painted in the middle of a white canvas is highly unified, but it  probably is not a good painting. The premise "A work which is unified, intense, and complex is always good" is not a true generalization either. The mere presence of some unity, complexity, and intensity does not ensure that the work which possesses them is good, only that the work has some good in it. So the fact, if it is a fact, that there are general principles of the sort Beardsley says there are and that deductive conclusions can be drawn from them does not mean that evaluation criticism can be reduced to a mechanical procedure. There is still the problem of deciding if the degree of unity, intensity, and complexity in a work is sufficient to make it a good work as distinct from a work which just has some good in it. Perhaps the only *strong* general principle in Beardsley's view that we could be sure is true is "A work which is highly unified, quite intense, and very complex is aways good."

Similar simplified deductive reconstructions of the reasoning of critics can be made with regard to matters other than unity. Beardsley mentions the use of humor in *Macbeth* (the drunken porter at the gate) to increase dramatic tension. A reconstruction of critical reasoning involving this point might go as follows:

| | |
|---|---|
| 1. An intense work always has some good in it. | Assumed premise |
| 2. There is a touch of humor in *Macbeth* which, together with other elements in the play, makes *Macbeth* intense. | By observation |
| 3. *Macbeth* is intense. | From 2 |
| 4. *Macbeth* has some good in it. | From 1 and 3 |

The reader can see how a reconstruction for complexity would go.

After it has been shown how Beardsley's theory of critical reasoning connects with his theory of value, an attempt will be made to formulate a deductive argument in which the conclusion states that a given work of art is good.

Of course, not every reason cited by a critic (a critic being anyone who talks about a work of art) in support of an evaluation is a good reason. Some "reasons" can be disqualified. From Beardsley's anti-intentionalist point of view, any attempt to support the goodness of a work because it fulfilled the artist's intention or the badness of it because it failed to realize the artist's intention is misguided. According to Beardsley, an artist's intention is not a part or aspect of the work of art, so any statement about it is irrelevant to the evaluation of a work. Also, not every statement which *is about* a work of art can be used to support an evaluation. Beardsley cites a writer who observed that Shakespeare used many hyphenated words and who maintained that the more hyphenated words in a poem the better poem it would be.[7] This contention is absurd. Consider also the neoclassical rule that the action of a play ought to take place within a period of twenty-four hours. This rule was presumably intended to embody a *primary* criterion, but it fails as a primary criterion because it clearly cannot be generalized to be applicable to all plays. However, it is possible to conceive of cases in which something like the twenty-four-hour limit would function as a secondary criterion. A given play might, for a variety of reasons, be very diffuse, and any change which would serve to make it more unified would make it better. In such a case, shortening the action to less than twenty-four hours *might* make the play more coherent and thus better.

Let us now turn to the instrumentalist theory of aesthetic value, which is supposed to provide the foundation for the general criterion theory. Following an old and widely held tradition, Beardsley maintains that a distinctive kind of experience can be isolated and described—aesthetic experience. Such experience is typically caused by aesthetic objects such as plays, paintings, poems, and the like, but may sometimes be caused by football games, sunsets, and so on. Aesthetic experience is the locus of aesthetic value.

Beardsley analyzes aesthetic experience in terms of five categories. The first characteristic belongs to the person undergoing the experience rather than the experience itself: such a person has his *attention firmly fixed* upon an object which controls the experience. His concentration contrasts with, say, the loose play of ideas in daydreaming. Second, the experience is marked by some *intensity* in which energies are focused on a rather narrow field of concern. This intensity may not be a full-blown emotion of the ordinary sort, but if the intensity does involve an emotion, it will be tied to some element of the aesthetic object. The concentrated intensity of the experience tends to shut out alien elements such as coughs in the theater, scratch noises on a record, thoughts of unpaid bills, and the like. Third, the aesthetic experience is *coherent*, or hangs together, to a relatively high degree. "One thing leads to another; continuity of development, without gaps or dead spaces, a sense of overall providential pattern of guidance, an orderly cumulation of energy toward a climax, are present to an unusual degree."[8] Fourth, the experience is *complete*. "The impulses and expectations aroused by elements within the experience are felt to be counterbalanced or resolved by other elements within the experience, so that some degree of equilibrium or finality is achieved and enjoyed. The experience detaches itself, and even insulates itself, from the intrusion of alien elements."[9] Coherence and completeness can be subsumed under *unity*. Aesthetic experience is quite unified; by contrast, ordinary experience is unorganized and diffuse. The fifth and last of the characteristics of aesthetic experience is *complexity*. "The range or diversity of distinct elements that . . .[the experience]. . .brings together into its unity, and under its dominant quality . . ."[10] is the measure of its complexity. The elements referred to here are the various affective and cognitive elements of the experience.

The characteristics of aesthetic experience turn out to be three in number: unity, intensity, and complexity. These, of course, are the same as the three primary criteria of critical reasoning. However, this is a parallelism and not an identification—these are related but distinct sets of things. Aesthetic objects have their various degrees of unity, intensity, and complexity which can be seen, heard, or understood (in, for example, literary work), and aesthetic experience has its unity,[11] intensity, and complexity. The unity, intensity, and complexity of aesthetic objects are perceived by someone and the perception of these qualities causes a further kind of unity, intensity, and complexity. For example, if I look at a painting and notice its unity (experience its unity), this in Beardsley's view can cause me to have unity of experience. In using the expression "unity of experience," I am trying to indicate that the caused unity is distinct from the unity perceived in the painting. The perceived intensity and complexity of an aesthetic object are also supposed to be able to cause intensity and complexity of experience. It is the causal relation between the elements of aesthetic objects and the elements of aesthetic experience which relate the general criterion theory of critical reasoning to the instrumentalist theory of aesthetic value.

Since each of the three elements of aesthetic experience can vary by degrees, a given experience may be more unified, more intense, or more complex than another. Thus two aesthetic experiences may be compared by the magnitudes of each of the three characteristics, but they may also be compared by the magnitudes of all three characteristics taken together. Of course, such magnitudes cannot be assigned exact mathematical measures, although in many cases it can be determined which of two experiences has the greater magnitude. What is important, however, is that it *can be determined* that a given experience has a greater or lesser magnitude, and this is what is significant for determining whether a certain aesthetic object is good or not.

At this point Beardsley makes an important observation and an important assumption. The *observation* is that aesthetic experience is a good thing. People would generally agree with Beardsley on this. Aesthetic experience may not be the best thing (the highest value), but it is a good thing. The *assumption* is that the greater the magnitude of an aesthetic experience, the better it is. It seems reasonable to assume this. The stage is now set for the definitions of "good aesthetic object" and "aesthetic value" which tie together Beardsley's theory of critical reasoning and his theory of aesthetic value. They are as follows:

> "X is a good aesthetic object" means "X is capable of producing aesthetic experiences (that is, aesthetic experiences of a fairly great magnitude) ."[12]

> "X has aesthetic value" means "X has the capacity to produce an aesthetic experience of a fairly great magnitude (such an experience having value) ."[13]

Note that the definitions are stated in terms of capacity, so that a good aesthetic object need not always produce a good aesthetic experience. Such an experience can only be produced when the object is experienced by someone who is susceptible (not color-blind, not tone-deaf, properly trained, and so on) . Note also that Beardsley's theory is complete and that he has not defined "good" or "value." These value terms appear on both sides of the final definitions. If Beardsley's theory is correct, he has succeeded in dealing with one of the most difficult questions that theories of aesthetic evaluation have to face, namely, the problem of defining "good."

With these definitions, Beardsley can now meet the challenge to the assumed premises of critical reasoning, for example, that a unified work always has some good in it. The reorganization of a whole deductive chain of critical evaluation might run as follows (considerations of intensity and complexity are omitted) :

1. A unified work can produce an aesthetic experience of some magnitude.

   From the argumentation that leads up to the definition of "good aesthetic object."

2. An aesthetic experience of some magnitude is good in some degree.

   By general agreement

3. A unified work can produce a thing which has some degree of good in it.

   From 1 and 2

| | |
|---|---|
| 4. Whatever can produce a thing with some degree of good is always (instrumentally) good in some degree. | By definition of terms (see below) |
| 5. A unified work is always (instrumentally) good in some degree. | From 3 and 4 |
| 6. This painting's colors are harmonious and its spatial design of planes and volumes is tightly organized. | By observation |
| 7. This painting is unified. | From 6 (or by observation) |
| 8. This painting is (instrumentally) good in some degree. | From 5 and 7 |

The addition of the premises from the theory of aesthetic value introduced an important change into the first premise of the critical reasoning (premise 5 here). It now turns out that the goodness of works of art is instrumental goodness. Philosophers distinguish between intrinsic goodness, which is good all by itself (independent of its relation to anything else), and instrumental goodness, which is the goodness that something has because it is a means to something else which is good. *A* might be instrumentally good because it produces *B*, which is intrinsically good, or *P* might be instrumentally good because it produces *Q*, which is itself also instrumentally good. The nature of the goodness referred to in premises 2 and 3 does not have to be known so far as Beardsley's theory of aesthetic evaluation is concerned. Beardsley maintains that all the goodness referred to in the premises is instrumental. It should be clear by now that in Beardsley's view, works of art are instrumentally good for producing aesthetic experiences which are themselves good things.

All the major elements and aspects of Beardsley's theory of evaluation have now been set forth, and a deductive reformulation of a critical evaluation which ends with the conclusion that a particular work of art is good can now be displayed.

1. A highly unified, quite intense, and very complex work can produce aesthetic experiences of a fairly great magnitude.

   From the argumentation that leads up to the definition of "good aesthetic object."

2. Aesthetic experiences of fairly great magnitude are good.

   By general agreement

3. A highly unified, quite intense, and very complex work can produce a thing which is good.

   From 1 and 2

4. Whatever can produce a thing which is good is always (instrumentally) good.

   By definition of terms

5. A highly unified, quite intense, and very complex work is always (instrumentally) good.

   From 3 and 4

6. This painting is highly unified, quite intense, and very complex.

   By observation

7. This painting is (instrumentally) good.

   From 5 and 6

Perhaps the greatest difficulty in applying this general scheme in actual cases of evaluation comes at the point of premise 2, where the question arises of deciding at what point of magnitude an aesthetic experience passes over the line from simply having some degree of good in it to having a large enough degree of good in it to be called "good." There are clear cases when the magnitude is great and when it is small, but the cases which fall in between are a problem, and the works which produce aesthetic experiences of intermediate magnitude are difficult to evaluate. However, this does not mean there is something wrong with the theory. The in-between cases are just difficult cases, and this kind of difficulty will naturally be reflected in an adequate theory of evaluation. A theory of evaluation should not be expected to solve the knotty problems of criticism but to show how and why they are knotty.

Beardsley's theory has the advantage of showing how the reason-giving of critics is a rational activity; it is deductive reasoning. (Inductive reasoning is used to support many of the premises of the deductive chain.) Some theories, however, maintain that criticism is not a rational activity, and we will examine these theories soon.

Beardsley's theory may at first glance seem to be unable to account for bad art, for he claims that every work of art has some aesthetic value. He argues that at worst a work might have zero intensity and complexity. Every work, however, will have at least a low degree of unity; therefore every work must have some aesthetic value. According to this view, a bad work is one with a low degree of aesthetic value and a good work is one with a high degree of aesthetic value. Thus Beardsley's theory can accommodate the full range of negative and positive aesthetic evaluations.

Earlier I indicated that philosophers typically work out their theories in terms of very basic value terms such as "good," "bad," and "aesthetic value." However, critics use a much richer evaluation vocabulary, and I promised to indicate how these richer terms should be analyzed. When a critic says, for example, that a work of art is magnificent or exquisite he is saying that it is good and is also giving an indication of the kind of features which make it good. In short, he is giving an evaluation plus an indication of his reasons. It is difficult to be precise in this matter, but when a critic says a work is magnificent, he is probably saying it is good and that it is large in scope in some respect. When a critic says a work is exquisite, he is probably saying it is good and that its details are intricately and carefully wrought. When a critic says a work is beautiful, he is clearly saying that it is good, but the word is used so broadly that it is difficult to know without more context what reasons, if any, are being suggested. On the negative side, when a critic writes, as one did write, that a play "is a mess," he is saying that it is bad and suggesting that it is disorganized, although admittedly the word "mess" is vague enough to leave room for many things. One could go on for a long time with specific evaluational words, but perhaps these are sufficient to indicate the way in which such words are to be analyzed.

## Chapter 17.  Other Theories of Evaluation

THERE ARE many accounts of evaluation besides instrumentalism, but because of the limitations of space I can discuss only the most important theories—important either because they have been widely held or because they have been philosophically prominent. Since the citing of reasons plays a significant role in actual criticism, attention will be given to the account each theory presents of reason-giving. Some of these theories make the giving of reasons irrelevant, but some do not. Six theories will be discussed. The view that I shall call 1) *subjectivism* proposes that reason-giving is essentially a pointless activity. The view I shall call 2) *Platonism 1* claims that reasons are unnecessary or not called for. The view I shall call 3) *Platonism 2* maintains that it is useful to give reasons, although they are always in principle dispensable. The view I shall call 4) *emotivism* maintains that evaluations cannot be *logically supported,* although "reasons" which *persuade* can be given. The view I shall call 5) *relativism* claims that there are principles and reasons but that ultimately the basic principles of criticism are *chosen* rather than justified. The view I shall call 6) *critical singularism* holds that reasons do not generate principles and consequently that there is no problem of justifying principles.

## Subjectivism

Subjectivism, unlike instrumentalism, attempts to *define* the basic evaluational term "aesthetic value" or "aesthetically good." What distinguishes subjectivism from other theories which try to define these expressions is that it attempts to define them in terms of the attitude of subjects, or persons. There are as many different possible versions of the subjectivist theory as there are ways of classifying persons. For example, the following would be a nonpersonal subjectivist definition: "aesthetically good" means "is liked (aesthetically) by all human beings." (The problem of how to distinguish aesthetic liking from liking in general is ignored here.) Such expressions as "is liked by upper-class people," "is liked by the proletariat," "is liked by my family," and so on, would also yield nonpersonal subjectivist definitions if anyone wished to use them to try to define the basic value term. However, because all versions of subjectivist theory face the same basic difficulties, I shall discuss only one.

It seems reasonable to discuss the most widely held subjectivist theory, namely, personal subjectivism, which asserts that "aesthetically good" means "is liked aesthetically by me." The word "me" in the definition refers, of course, to whichever speaker utters a sentence which contains the phrase "aesthetically good" or a synonym for it. According to this theory, "aesthetically good" contains an implicit reference to any person who uses the expression. This view has been held by some philosophers[14] and held or assumed in a less conscious and explicit way by many people. Henceforth, I shall use the term "subjectivism" to refer to the personal "liked by me" variety of subjectivism. If I wish to refer to any other variety, I will so specify.

There are a number of reasons why this definition seems plausible. First, there is a close and important relation between the goodness of an aesthetic object and liking it. Of course, the fact that there is a close relation does not mean that the relation is that of the identity of meaning. For example, the relation might be that it is desirable that whatever is judged aesthetically good be liked. Second, what has been called "the whirligig of taste"—the change in what is thought good in art from age to age, the fact that what is thought good in art by a person has frequently varied during

the person's lifetime, and so on—gives comfort to subjectivism. If subjectivism is true, then one would expect that what
is held to be good would vary widely, since it is admitted by
all that  likings are subject to wide variation. Nevertheless,
it is clear that such variation of taste does not *prove* subjectivism true. A number of things might account for the variation—immaturity, being uninformed, and so on, in the
cases of the changes both in a particular individual and in
many individuals of a certain period.

From a logical point of view, subjectivism has an interesting consequence: it makes critical disputes impossible. Suppose two critics, Jones and Smith, are disputing about a
painting. Jones claims the painting is good and Smith claims
it is not. The dispute has the appearance of being about the
painting, but if subjectivism is true, they are not talking in a
straightforward way about the painting and there is no dispute. If "good" means "is liked by me," then when Jones
says the painting is good he is saying, "I (Jones) like the
painting," and when Smith says the painting is not good, he
is saying, "I (Smith) do not like the painting." The statements "Jones likes the painting" and "Smith does not like
the painting" can both be true at the same time without any
conflict. The two statements are not about the same thing.
(Some forms of subjectivism do not have this consequence.
If "good" means "is liked by the majority of the human
race," then if Jones and Smith disagree, they are at least
talking about the same things and in principle the dispute
could be settled by a large-scale inquiry into the likes of
human beings.)

The considerations which make subjectivism plausible are
clearly not conclusive reasons for thinking it true; and if it
were true, critical dispute would have a different logical
structure than seems to be presupposed by the activity and
remarks of critics—disputing critics seem to think that they
are arguing about the same thing and not simply asserting
their own likings. There are several arguments which show
that subjectivism is probably false.

The first argument is really an expansion of the above remark about the logical structure of critical disputes. Critics almost always give reasons to support their evaluation, and we often find such reasons helpful in understanding the evaluations and in deciding whether we think the evaluations justified or not. In the first place, it does not make much sense to say that evaluations are justified or unjustified, if "good" is identical in meaning with "liking." Ordinarily we do not justify our likings—they just are. If asked to justify why I like ice cream, I might say, "Because it is sweet." But this is just a way of saying I *like* sweet things or of being more specific about what it is *about* ice cream I like. If asked to justify why I like a painting, I might point out various of its aspects which I like. But all this seems very different from the justification of evaluations. Still, the subjectivist will no doubt find these remarks beside the point. He will say that these remarks only make sense because it is assumed that subjectivism is false and that begs the whole question.

A second argument against subjectivism derives from the fact that we sometimes admit that we like something we judge not to be good. Furthermore, we sometimes judge something good but do not like it. Neither of these two would be possible if subjectivism were true. For example, if subjectivism were true and we liked something, it would be impossible not to judge it good, and similar considerations apply to the second case. It must be noted parenthetically that this argument does not necessarily apply to nonpersonal versions of subjectivism, in which "good" is not defined in terms of a particular person's likes. The subjectivist might still reply that we only *think* that we are making the kinds of judgments cited and that we are confused about our language.

The third argument against subjectivism is G. E. Moore's open-question argument—discussed in Chapter 7—which is supposed to prove that *no* definition of "good" can be given.[15] Formulated against subjectivism, the argument runs as follows. If "aesthetically good" means "is liked aesthetically by me," then an evaluation of a work of art such as "This painting is good" is equivalent in meaning to the state-

ment "This painting is liked by me." The open-question
argument maintains that when one is faced with statements
such as "This painting is liked by me," one can *always* sensi-
bly ask, "Yes, I understand that you like the painting, but is
it a good painting?" If subjectivism were true, such a question would be silly, for it would reduce to "Yes, I understand that you like the painting, but do you like the painting?" Since the question is not silly, subjectivism must be
false. However, the subjectivist might point out, as some
philosophers have done against Moore, that the general ap-
plicability of the open-question argument presupposes the
truth of Moore's own view that "good" cannot be defined
and names a simple unanalyzable, nonnatural property. The
subjectivist can maintain that 1) it is true that the application of the open-question argument shows that many definitions of "good" are incorrect, but 2) it only shows that all
definitions are wrong if Moore's theory is true and that has
not been proven, and that 3) subjectivism is in fact true.

However, the open-question argument does suggest a conclusive line of argument against subjectivism. This argument
depends upon our careful reflection on how we use language,
specifically evaluational language and language used to describe our psychological states. Even though we may not be
able to give a complete analysis of what "good" means or how
we use the term, it is clear that it is not identical in meaning
with "is liked by me" or for that matter with any phrase of
the "is liked by" type. Saying something is good and saying
something is liked play two very different roles in our linguistic activities. Briefly, to say that something is good is to
say that it has satisfied certain standards; to say that something is liked is to make a statement about a psychological
fact. We use statements about goodness to do one kind of
job and statements about likes to do quite a different kind
of job.

As a last resort, the subjectivist might say that his theory is
not about the way that we actually use language now but that
he is attempting to *reform* language in order to give us a
better way to talk. He might claim that his reform would give
us a simple and straightforward way of verifying our evalua-

tions—I can verify if something is good by discovering if I like it. Such attempts at reform are misguided, however, for the main purpose of a theory of evaluation is to throw light on and explain the practice of critical reasoning and evaluation that is part of our ordinary linguistic behavior. It is true that a great deal of nonsense is spoken about art and the evaluation of art, but surely the whole practice of evaluating art and the basic terms of the practice are not in need of radical reform. The subjectivist's "reform" reduces the whole business of the evaluation of art to the liking of art, which virtually eliminates the need of giving reasons for evaluations. The reform simply dismisses rather than explains what needs to be explained.

## Platonism 1

Both Platonism 1 and Platonism 2 have their origins in Plato's theory of beauty, and both are similar in important ways to some present-day theories of evaluation, for example, the theory of G. E. Moore.[16] And some such theory as Platonism 1 or Platonism 2 is presupposed by critics and ordinary persons who think that properly made critical evaluations are absolute, that is, that critical evaluations are true in a way which makes no reference to the psychological states of subjects. However, I am not claiming that either Platonism 1 or Platonism 2 is Plato's or Moore's theory; they are simply generalized statements of the type of theory of which Plato's and Moore's theories are instances.

Platonism 1 maintains that in addition to their natural or empirical properties such as being of a certain color, size, and shape, or consisting of certain tones, sounds, and so on, works of art and natural objects may also possess a nonnatural or nonempirical value property, variously referred to by such terms as "beauty," "aesthetic value," and "aesthetic goodness." There may be nonempirical properties such as *moral goodness* and perhaps others which relate more directly to aesthetics, but this discussion will be concerned only with *beauty*. According to Platonism 1, the nonempirical property of beauty is unanalyzable and therefore indefinable. That is, the word "beauty" denotes a logically primitive entity which cannot be analyzed into parts in the way that, say, "man" supposedly can be analyzed into *rational* and *animal*. The meaning of beauty cannot be conveyed to someone by a definition or a verbal description, and the meaning of the word "beauty" can be learned only by experiencing beauty. In this respect, the term "beauty" is supposed to be like an empirical color term such as "red," the meaning of which, it is generally maintained, can only be learned by experiencing the empirical property of redness. Empirical properties and the nonempirical property of beauty are apprehended by different modes of knowing: empirical properties are perceived and known by the ordinary modes of sense perception —sight, hearing, touch, and the like—while nonempirical or trancendental properties are apprehended by an entirely different way of knowing called "intuition." Intuition, of course, depends on the ordinary modes of knowing in the sense that the ordinary modes must provide the mind with information about the empirical properties of an object before the mind can intuit whether or not the object also possesses the trancendental property of beauty and to what degree. But whereas ordinary perception is sensuous, intuition is not. It is this contention of Platonism 1 that the object of intuition is not an empirical property or set of empirical properties which makes intuitionism (ethical or aesthetic) so controversial and so endlessly debated. The lack of an empirical check on the correctness or incorrectness of particular alleged intuitions is the root of the controversy.

The most attractive feature of Platonism 1 is that the theory furnishes us with an objective way of evaluating works of art. There is much unresolved disagreement over what works are aesthetically good or beautiful, and Platonism 1 promises that such disputes are in theory resolvable. According to it, beauty is a property of an object and is *there* to be experienced by anyone who has the capacity to apprehend it. Beauty is as objective a property of a thing as is its color or size, although it is not known in the same way that color and size are known. If Platonism 1 is true, in a dispute about whether or not an object is beautiful, one of the disputants must be right and one wrong, because an object either has the property of beauty or it does not. A person who is wrong in such a dispute, according to the theory, is blind to beauty (although perhaps not in all cases), i.e., lacks the intuitive power to apprehend beauty in the case in question. By the way, it is of course possible, given the theory, that a person can correctly claim that an object possesses beauty and yet lack the capacity to know that it does—he can correctly guess that it possesses beauty or claim that it does on the authority of someone who has the relevant capacity.

To flesh out Platonism 1 more completely, it can be noted that a person might have the capacity to intuit beauty in certain kinds of art, say, paintings, and not have the capacity in the case of other kinds of art, say, music. The capacity might be even more limited in a given person; for example, a person might be able to intuit the beauty in representational paintings but not in nonobjective paintings. This point makes clear that the capacity to intuit beauty claimed by Platonism 1 is not a simple, easily obtained ability. Some persons might not possess it at all, and some persons might possess the capacity to intuit beauty but not develop the abilities to discriminate acutely in connection with empirical properties and their relations. In order to intuit beauty in paintings, one must learn to discriminate between subtle colors, learn to be aware of composition, and so on. Similar considerations hold for the other arts. In short, in order to bring out our ability to intuit beauty, we must first develop many other abilities.

Another characteristic of Platonism 1 is that it supposes that beauty is intuited on a case-by-case basis and that no general conclusions follow from the cases of beauty experienced. For example, all the paintings which possess the nonempirical property of beauty need not have any empirical property in common. And if, in fact, it turned out that all existing beautiful paintings do have one or a set of empirical properties in common, all the beautiful paintings which subsequently may come into existence might very well not have that property or set of properties. According to Platonism 1, the capacity to intuit beauty is always necessary in order to know that a given work of art or natural object possesses beauty. There are no empirical indices which persons who lack the capacity can use to identify objects which possess beauty. The intuiting of beauty is analogous to the perceiving of a particular color, say, red. There is no *perceptual* property other than redness that all red things have in common, so there is no perceptual index which a color-blind person who cannot distinguish red can use to infer that something is red or not. If it were the case that all red things were square and all square things were red, then the color-blind person would be able to infer which things are red and which are not because even though he could not discriminate red, he could discriminate squareness.

With one, perhaps trivial, exception, reason-giving is not possible if Platonism 1 is true. Given this theory, the proposition which would have to be supported by reasons would be of the general type "X is beautiful." However, according to the theory, there is nothing which is correlated with beauty, so there is nothing other than beauty which can serve as a reason for thinking a thing beautiful. The only "reason" for thinking a thing beautiful is knowing that it possesses beauty by way of intuition. The trivial exception alluded to is the case in which it is known that X is beautiful and Y is exactly similar to X in all its properties and in all the relations among its properties (perhaps Y is an absolutely faithful copy of X). In this case, it could be said that the fact that Y is exactly similar to X and X is beautiful is a reason for thinking that Y possesses beauty.

## Platonism 2

Platonism 2 is identical with Platonism 1 except in one regard. In Chapter 2 it was noted that Plato maintained that all beautiful things have the always accompanying property of *unity*. Thus, in Plato's view, if something is unified, then there is some, though not conclusive, reason to think that it may be beautiful. However, the view that I am calling Platonism 2 makes an even stronger claim than that of historical Platonism; it maintains that all beautiful things have a certain empirical property $A$ and that everything that has the empirical property $A$ is beautiful. It is not necessary to specify what empirical property $A$ is; it is sufficient to say that Platonism 2 maintains that there is such a property and that one can discover which empirical property is the beauty-related property.

If true, Platonism 2 has an important advantage over Platonism 1: it is possible for persons who do not possess the capacity to intuit beauty to know which things are beautiful and which are not. Once those who can intuit beauty discover the identity of property $A$, then all that anyone has to do to know which things are beautiful is to determine which things possess property $A$. Thus, for example, a beauty-blind person could select and fill his home with beautiful things for people to enjoy, although he himself would not be able to enjoy their beauty. He would know that the things were beautiful, but he could not appreciate their beauty.

According to Platonism 2, the fact that a thing possesses property $A$ is a conclusive reason in support of the contention that that thing is beautiful. Such reason-giving would be helpful in establishing the truth of a conclusion that a particular thing is beautiful, but it would be of especial importance in a certain kind of case. Suppose that a particular work of art is especially complicated and subtle so that the process of experiencing and studying it in order to intuit and appreciate its beauty would be arduous and time-consuming. The time and effort necessary to determine if the work of art possessed beauty would be great, and if it turned out that the work did not possess beauty, the time and effort would have been wasted. However, it *might* be relatively easy to discover if the work had the empirical property $A$, and if it did, then one could be assured in advance that the time devoted to the work would be rewarding. Thus, for Platonism 2, reason-giving (citing property $A$) has a certain value. However, in the case of persons who possess the capacity to intuit beauty, such reason-giving is in principle dispensable. For such persons, beauty can always be experienced directly so that it is unnecessary (although sometimes convenient) to have recourse to giving reasons that something is beautiful.

One danger that Platonism 2 faces is the logical possibility that a beautiful thing will turn up which does not possess property $A$. If such a case turned up, property $A$ could no longer function as a conclusive reason, although the possession of property $A$ by an object would still be a reason for thinking that the object probably is beautiful.

As noted earlier, the most attractive feature of Platonism 1 and Platonism 2 is that they promise an objective way of settling disputes in aesthetic matters. However, the assurance of objectivity is purchased at a very high price. The basis of the objectivity is the alleged nonempirical, indefinable property of beauty which, since it is nonempirical, must be known by a special mode of knowing—intuition. First, the knowledge and appreciation of beauty is available only to an elite whose members have the capacity to intuit it. This objection, however, is not a criticism of the truth of the theory but only states an inconvenient aspect of it. Second, many people are suspicious of intuition as a mode of knowlege: it seems so tailor-made to solve a given problem in aesthetics. Intuition is supposed to be a mode of knowlege which has but one object—beauty. Admittedly, there is a parallel moral theory which maintains that intutition has moral goodness as its object, but even so, the number of types of objects of intuition is embarrassingly small when compared with the great multitude of objects of ordinary empirical knowledge. It is easy to see how intuition could be abused and used as a refuge for knowledge claims which cannot really be substantiated, and this makes people suspicious. Nevertheless, it is not possible to prove that intuitionism is false. The intuitionist can always argue that anyone who disputes his claim simply lacks the capacity to intuit beauty (or to intuit moral goodness if the intuitionist is defending moral intuitionism) . By the very nature of his claim, the intuitionist puts his theory outside the range of refutation; still, this fact does not prove his theory true, nor does it inspire confidence in it.

## Emotivism

The emotive theory is an account of evaluation which arose within logical positivism, a philosophical movement which had great influence in the period from about 1930 to 1950. Logical positivism claims that all knowledge is either empirical, as are the truths of science, or tautological, as are the truths of pure mathematics. Logical positivism flatly rejects the claim of intuitionism that there are nonempirical, nontautological truths which state moral and aesthetic evaluations and which are known to be true by means of intuition. The logical positivist considers intuition a philosophical device invented to give moral and aesthetic evaluations the appearance of being truths.

A. J. Ayer, a British philosopher, formulated a well-known statement of emotivism in 1936, and the account given here is based on his views.[17] Ayer rejects Moore's and all other versions of intuitionism as unempirical, but he adopts Moore's open-question argument against all attempts to define the basic evaluation terms. Ayer formulates his version of the open-question argument against both subjectivism and hedonism, which he apparently takes to be typical of theories attempting to define "good" or some other moral word in terms of empirical notions. Having shown, he thinks, that subjectivism and hedonism are incorrect, he assumes that the same argument can be used successfully against any attempt to define "good."

Let us consider his argument against hedonism. The hedonistic view he attacks claims that good can be defined in terms of pleasure, i.e., that the word "good" is identical in meaning with the word "pleasure" or with some varient of it such as "pleasant." Thus, "X is good" has the same meaning as "X is pleasant," according to this theory. The great advantage of hedonism is that if it is correct, then moral and aesthetic evaluations are really empirical propositions about pleasure and can be verified or falsified. The theory of evaluation turns out to be a part of empirical psychology. Unfortunately for hedonism, Ayer claims, it is not self-contradictory to say, claim, or hold that there are some pleasant things which are not good, i.e., to hold that some pleasant things are bad. If hedonism were true, i.e., if "good" and "pleasant" were identical in meaning, then it would be self-contradictory to say that some pleasures are not good. That is, if hedonism were true, then we would be able to substitute "good" for "pleasure" in the sentence "Some pleasures are not good" and the self-contradictory sentence "Some goods are not good" would result. However, since "Some pleasures are not good" is not self-contradictory, hedonism must be false. Ayer uses exactly the same argument against subjectivism.

What criterion is Ayer using in saying that "Some pleasures are not good" is not self-contradictory? If someone said, "Some bachelors are married," we would say that the sentence is self-contradictory because of the way in which we use or understand the word "bachelor." In other words, part of the meaning of "bachelor," as we use the term, is unmarriedness. In short, the inconsistency of a given sentence in a given language is shown by appealing to the meanings of the terms in that language. What Ayer is maintaining, then, is that the subjectivist and hedonist definitions do not comprehend the diversity of ways in which we use such terms as "good" in English or any other natural language. His method is to find a sentence which seems perfectly sensible to ordinary users of English and to show that the sentence would be inconsistent given a certain definition. Ayer's most general claim is that he can produce a counter-instance sentence for any proposed definition of basic value terms. This claim is justified only if it can somehow be "seen" that the uses of "good" and other such terms in English are so diverse that no definition could encompass them.

Ayer asserts that of course we could construct a language in which the hedonist definition is adequate or a language in which the subjectivist definition is adequate, but neither of these languages would be English and English is the language in which we make our moral and aesthetic evaluations. So far as ethics and aesthetics are concerned at least, Ayer is an "ordinary language" philosopher. That is, he maintains that ordinary language usage is the criterion for the correctness or incorrectness of definitions.

If "good" or any other basic value term does not refer to a primitive, unanalyzable property known by intuition or cannot be defined in terms which refer to empirical properties, then how does "good" function? It would seem that all the ways have been ruled out in which "good" could function in a sentence by *referring* to something by virtue of which the sentence would be true or false. Ayer's conclusion is that evaluative sentences are not capable of being either true or false and that evaluative terms simply serve to express the feelings—pro or con—of the persons who use them. According to Ayer, when a person says of a painting he is looking at, "This painting is beautiful," the person is not asserting or saying something about the painting, he is simply expressing his pro feelings about the painting. Uttering the sentence in question amounts to saying, "This painting—hurrah!" The sentence "This is a bad painting" amounts to "This painting—bah!" Ayers' theory is sometimes referred to as the Bah-Hurrah Theory.

There is some danger of confusing Ayer's view with the version of subjectivism which wants to define "good" in terms of "is liked by me." However, according to this version of subjectivism, "X is good" means "X is liked by me," and the latter is either true or false; evaluative terms refer and evaluative sentences assert something about the world which is either true or false. According to emotivism, however, evaluative terms are simply expressive, and evaluative sentences do *not* assert anything. However, there is a respect in which emotivism is similar to the "liked by me" version of subjectivism. If two persons disagree, one saying, "This painting is beautiful" and the other saying, "This painting is not beautiful," the disagreement is only apparent and not real. The first person is expressing his pro attitude toward the painting and the second is expressing his con attitude toward the painting, but neither is really *asserting* anything. Since nothing is being asserted by either person, there is no disagreement. The impossibility of disagreement over evaluations contrasts with the disagreements we can have over facts. For example, if two persons disagree about, say, the color of an object, each is making an assertion or a claim about a feature of the empirical world. And, of course, it is possible in principle to settle a dispute over facts. However, according to emotivism, a disagreement over values cannot be settled by discovering some proposition to be true.

Nevertheless, disagreement over values can be resolved in the sense that as the result of a debate, a closer look at the painting, a threat, flattery, or whatever, one of the parties may experience a change in attitude. Also, according to Ayer, attitudes may be influenced directly by the uttering of evaluational sentences. When Jones says, "This painting is beautiful," he not only expresses his feelings toward the painting, but he may excite pro feelings in others. It is possible, then, that the mere uttering of an evaluational sentence may bring about sameness of attitude or feeling.

To give a *reason* in criticism is to cite some feature of a work of art in support of an evaluational statement about the work, that is, to make a statement which is evidence that the evaluation is true. Since emotivism claims that evaluations are not capable of being either true or false, there is no straightforward way of giving reasons if emotivism is true. If a critic says that a play is bad because it is tedious, he is not, according to emotivism, giving a reason for the truth of "The play is bad," although knowledge of the tediousness of the play may make someone adopt a con attitude toward it. However, if critics cannot, according to emotivism, give reasons for evaluation, they can give what might be called "persuaders." An important consequence of this feature of emotivism is that whereas those philosophers who support reason-giving distinguish between good and bad reasons, there is no way to distinguish between good and bad persuaders. Anything that a critic might say or do—cite a feature of a work of art, make a threat of bodily harm, kick someone—might result in someone having a change of attitude. If, however, there is no distinction between good and bad persuaders from the point of view of being evidence for the *truth* of evaluative conclusions and anything may function as a persuader, then evaluative criticism is clearly not a rational activity. Of course, one persuader may be more effective than another, but this sense of betterness and worseness does not have anything to do with the truth of evaluations in the emotive view.

An important criticism of Ayer's version of emotivism is that its analysis of evaluation is too simple. A number of later emotivists attempted to remedy this defect by arguing that evaluations have a descriptive aspect and perhaps an imperative aspect as well. The best known of these emotivist analyses is C. L. Stevenson's *Ethics and Language*.[18] Some of the central features of emotivism will reappear in relativism, the next evaluational theory to be discussed.

## Relativism

The view that I am calling "relativism" is an adaptation of some of the basic features of the moral philosophy of R. M. Hare[19] to the problem of evaluation in criticism. Relativism is similar to the view of Bernard Heyl.[20] In some ways, relativism is also similar to Beardsley's theory of criticism, although it does not affirm his instrumentalist theory of value.

The logical foundation of relativism lies in the type of analysis which Hare gives of good. This analysis purports to be a description of our use of the term "good" in both moral and nonmoral contexts: Hare claims that "good" functions in the same way regardless of context. If Hare is right, there would seem to be no reason why an account of "good work of art" cannot be formulated.

Hare, like Ayer, uses a version of Moore's open-question argument to show that no descriptive term or terms such as "pleasant," "I approve," or the like has the *same meaning* as "good." Consequently, no set of statements consisting only of descriptions of something can *entail* that something is good. But whereas Ayer makes no serious attempt to discover how evaluative language actually works and quickly concludes that "good" does not have any cognitive meaning and is merely expressive of feelings, Hare examines evaluative language carefully and at great length and concludes that the meaning of "good" is its *commending* function. He claims 1) that what is common to all normal uses of "good" in any context is that a commendation is being made and 2) that there is nothing else common to such uses. Hare's claim is clearly about how we use evaluative words; like Ayer, he is an ordinary-language philosopher on this point. Hare distinguishes between *the meaning* of "good," which is not context-dependent, and *the criteria* of "good," which are. Although we always commend when we use "good," the criteria we use when applying "good" vary from context to context. In both cases, when we say "That is a good watch" and "That is a good radio," we are commending, but we use one set of criteria for watches and another set for radios. The characteristics which make a radio good are different from those that make a watch good.

The evaluation of watches and radios is relatively easy and straightforward because there is widespread agreement about the criteria of goodness for watches and radios. The same cannot be said about morals and art criticism, so it is a good idea to illustrate the theory first with easy examples. Consider what is involved in correctly saying, "This is a good watch." First, one is commending a particular watch. Second, one is affirming that a particular watch satisfies all (or some sufficient set) of the criteria of good watches. If the evaluation is challenged, the person who made the evaluation is committed to giving justifying *reasons,* that is, to *showing* that the watch satisfies the criteria for goodness in watches. As reasons, it might be pointed out that the watch keeps accurate time, is small in size, and so on. It is important to note that in asserting that something is a good watch, one is *committing* oneself to a certain criterion or certain criteria and thereby to a principle which embodies the criterion or criteria. Thus, if one judges a particular watch *A* to be good, then one is committed to saying of any watch exactly like *A* that it is good also. Of course, exact likeness is not required in the case of watches (and in the great majority of other things) because certain features, for example, shape in most instances, are irrelevant to goodness in watches. Hare, like Beardsley, claims that evaluation is a *deductive* procedure involving general principles. This feature may be illustrated as follows:

1. All watches which have properties *A, B,* and *C* are good.
2. This watch has properties *A, B,* and *C*.
3. Therefore, this watch is good.

The contention that evaluation is a deductive procedure from general principles is really identical with the contention that saying that *X* is good commits the sayer to a general principle of goodness for things of type *X*. The first way of formulating the contention starts "at the top" with given or established principles from which the particular evaluation is deduced. The second way of formulating the contention starts "at the bottom" with the particular evaluation that one wishes to make; the making of the particular evaluation *generates* the general principle for all relevantly similar cases. We start at the top when evaluating such things as watches and radios for which there are established principles of goodness which every evaluator accepts. We start at the bottom when we wish or find it necessary to evaluate something for which there are no established principles or the person making the evaluation rejects the established principles. The fact, if it is a fact, that starting at the bottom generates and commits one to general principles which cover all relevantly similar cases shows that evaluative language cannot be used lightly.

The function of principles, whether moral, critical, or

otherwise, is to furnish a rational framework for evaluation. Because of their generality, principles provide a stability which might not be achievable if one proceeded from case to case without trying to relate the cases in any way. Also, principles can be taught in the sense that one person can state a principle for another and the hearer can understand it. There is, of course, no guarantee that the hearer will accept as a principle what he hears and understands. Principles provide a procedure for helping to ensure consistency; that is, insofar as a critic uses principles, he will treat similar cases similarly. To say of two exactly similar cases that one is good and the other bad would be a case of inconsistency. It is worth noting that an individual may not be able to formulate explicitly the principles that he holds and uses. The test of whether or not a person uses principles in his evaluating is whether or not he evaluates cases similarly that are similar in the relevant respects. A person's evaluations may satisfy this test without his realizing that they do; one does not have to understand about principles in an abstract way in order to have and employ principles. In fact, person *B* may learn from person *A* to use a principle in a given context by observing *A*'s particular evaluations without either *A* or *B* being able to formulate the principle which has been passed on.

By now it should be clear that the logical structure of relativism as developed thus far is the same as that of Beardsley's general criterion theory. However, whereas Beardsley attempts to supply a content for the logical structure by maintaining that unity, intensity, and complexity are primary criteria of goodness, Hare is content with describing the logical structure of evaluation, moral, critical, or otherwise. Hare's lack of attempt to supply substantive highest-order (primary) principles is not due to any fault in his theory but rather to his view of the logical status of such principles. We have seen that Beardsley thinks his substantive primary principles can be justified by an appeal to their utility in producing good aesthetic experiences. However, according to relativism, the highest-order principles of criticism cannot themselves be justified—they are themselves the ultimate grounds of aesthetic justification. What, then, can be said of the primary principles of criticism which people hold and use? Relativism's answer is that highest-order principles come to be held as the result of the *decision* of the holder. The decision may be a conscious one or it may be a result of "picking it up" from one's cultural environment. Hare calls both of these ways of coming to hold a principle "decisions" because both are cases of accepting a principle without deducing it from already held premises or without inducing it as probable from premises. Principles are neither true nor false; they simply embody decisions to commend certain types of things.

Beardsley and Hare agree that criteria (and hence principles) are necessarily involved with goodness. They *may* differ over the meaning of "good": Beardsley gives no account of good, but Hare argues that the meaning of "good" is its use to commend. According to Hare, commending is an action done by an individual on his own initiative and from his own principles, and one can decide to commend or not to commend. Criteria and principles go together to produce generality, commending and decision go together to relate the generality to an individual person. It is the decision aspect which provides a means for change in or of principles. One changes a principle by deciding (consciously or not) to commend in a different way from the way one has in the past, that is, by predicating "good" on the basis of different criteria.

It would, of course, be possible for a particular relativist, call him "Jones," to decide for Beardsley's substantive principles of unity, intensity, and complexity. If this were done, then the logical structure and content of Jones's theory and Beardsley's theory would be the same, although they would still differ on the question of the justification of the highest-order principles of critical evaluation. However, given the relativist point of view, no one is bound to agree with Jones and Beardsley, and it is at least possible for each person to have a different set of critical principles. It would also be consistent with relativism if everyone were to agree on the same set of critical principles. What makes a view relativistic is that its highest-order principles are not themselves justified but are decided for.

A critical relativist, call him "Smith," would cease to be a relativist if he could establish his highest-order critical principles not by decision but by deriving them from some other principles. Beardsley does something like this in trying to justify his primary critical principles with his instrumentalist theory of value. If Smith attempts to justify his primary critical principles, they will still be his highest-order *critical* principles but not his highest-order principles—the critical principles will be subservient to some higher principles.

If the relativists are correct about the logical status of critical principles, are there any considerations which might be kept in mind when deciding on principles and which might tend to result in general agreement on principles? Perhaps the best that can be said in this regard is that critics should be widely acquainted with the arts to which they apply their critical principles. However, if the past is any guide, there seems to be scant hope that even well-informed critics will agree completely. Still, there is nothing which rules out the possibility of widespread or even complete agreement. I suspect, however, that many relativists see the possibility of complete agreement as a stagnant situation in which both art and criticism would have lost their vitality.

## Critical Singularism

A number of philosophers in recent years have argued that principles play no role in the criticism of art.[21] These philosophers agree that critics do give reasons and that to do so is a proper function of criticism, but they maintain that a reason does not involve a principle. They contrast reason-giving in criticism with reason-giving in morality and in the evaluation of such things as watches and radios. To give a reason to justify an act as morally right or a watch as good involves a principle, but works of art, they contend, are very different from moral actions and watches. In fact, the difference is so great that works of art cannot be evaluated at all. Critical singularism is an evaluational theory in that it is an account of how evaluational language functions when applied to art, but it maintains that such language when applied to art serves no evaluational purpose. When a critic says of a work of art that it is good and gives a reason for saying so, the reason does not serve to justify calling the work "good." According to the critical singularist, the reason functions to call some quality of the work of art to the attention of the person who reads or hears the critic's remark. Once attention has been called to a quality of a work, the reader or hearer can appreciate that quality, if he can discriminate it. Evaluative terms simply play a role in a process the sole function of which is to call attention to the various qualities of works of art.

Critical singularists seem to rely on two arguments in rejecting the relevance of principles in art criticism: 1) that a quality cited as a merit (a reason) in one work of art may not be a merit or may even be a defect in another work of art and that, consequently, there cannot be a general principle involving such a quality applicable to all works of art and 2) that works of art are unique and that, consequently, it is impossible to say that one work is better than another—each work of art is in a class by itself, and it is senseless to try to compare one work with another.

As we have seen in Chapter 16, Beardsley attempts to deal with the first argument by saying that not every reason generates a principle, and he distinguishes between primary and secondary criteria. In Beardsley's view, there are only three primary principles.

The first problem with the argument about uniqueness is to find out what is intended. Every object or event is unique in the sense that it is just the thing it is, but this cannot be what the critical singularists have in mind because they wish to say that works of art are unique in a way that other things are not. Perhaps they wish to maintain that every work of art is different in some respect from every other work of art; in this sense, works of art would contrast with a mass-produced series of watches each of which is exactly like the other. Even so, at least Beardsley would argue, works of art are similar in that each is more or less unified, intense, and complex.

Mary Mothersill, although she rejects the uniqueness argument,[22] defends critical singularism and argues that such canons, or primary principles, as Beardsley advances are arbitrary.[23] She asks, "Aren't there 'satisfactory works of art' which are *disunified?*" and then goes on to cite some works which are supposedly both good and disunified. However, in Beardsley's case at least, the absence of one primary criterion does not make a work bad. Neither, of course, would the presence of only one of the primary criteria make a work good. As we saw in the account of Beardsley's view, even the primary criteria are interrelated, and one cannot focus on a single criterion and draw a conclusion about a work. As for the charge of arbitrariness, Beardsley could attempt to answer the charge with his account of aesthetic experience and his instrumentalist theory of aesthetic value, but it is not clear how the relativist can deal with the charge. A relativist might try to develop a response by talking in terms of the pervasiveness in works of art of the characteristics which his critical principles embody. There is not space to deal with this problem here but it is worth noting that critical singularism itself is not entirely immune from the charge of arbitrariness. According to critical singularism, critics simply draw our attention to certain qualities of works of art, but the theory provides no justification for choosing one quality rather than another to draw attention to and this seems arbitrary.

It is clear that the problems involved in the evaluation of art are far from being resolved and that widespread philosophical disagreement persists. I believe, however, that at least some of the philosophizing discussed here in Part V has significantly advanced our knowledge of evaluation, and there is promise that further progress can be made in the future.

# Notes

## Part I

1. Monroe Beardsley, *Aesthetics from Classical Greece to the Present* (New York: Macmillan, 1966).
2. Jerome Stolnitz, "On the Significance of Lord Shaftesbury in Modern Aesthetic Theory," *The Philosophical Quarterly* (1961), pp. 97–113.
3. Stolnitz, "Beauty: Some Stages in the History of an Idea," *Journal of the History of Ideas* (1961), pp. 185–204.
4. Stolnitz, "On the Origins of 'Aesthetic Disinterestedness,'" *The Journal of Aesthetics and Art Criticism* (1961), pp. 131–143.
5. Walter J. Hipple, Jr., *The Beautiful, the Sublime, and the Picturesque in Eighteenth-Century British Aesthetic Theory* (Carbondale, Ill.: Southern Illinois U. P., 1957).
6. Plato, *Symposium*, trans. W. Hamilton (Baltimore: Penguin Books, 1951).
7. Plato, *Philibus and Epinomis*, trans. A. E. Taylor (London: Nelson, 1956).
8. Plotinus, *The Enneads*, trans. S. MacKenna (London: Faber and Faber, 1966).
9. Thomas Aquinas, *Basic Writings of St. Thomas Aquinas*, vol. I, trans. (New York: Random House, 1945), p. 46 and elsewhere.
10. Marsilio Ficino, *Commentary on Plato's Symposium*, trans. S. R. Jayne (Columbia, Mo.: University of Missouri Studies, 1944).
11. Leon Battista Alberti, *On Painting*, trans. J. R. Spencer (Yale U. P., 1956); *On Architecture*, trans. J. Leoni (1726), facsimile ed. (London: 1955).
12. Alexander Baumgarten, *Reflections on Poetry* (1735).
13. Shaftesbury, *Characteristics of Men, Manners, Opinions, Times*, vol. II, J. M. Robertson, ed. (Indianapolis: Bobbs-Merrill, 1964), p. 126.
14. *Loc. cit.*
15. Shaftesbury, *op. cit.*, pp. 127–8.
16. Francis Hutcheson, *An Inquiry into the Original of Our Ideas of Beauty and Virtue*, 2nd ed. (London: 1726), p. 7.
17. *Ibid.*, p. 11.

18. Edmund Burke, *A Philosophical Enquiry into the Origin of Our Ideas of the Sublime and Beautiful,* 6th ed. (London: 1770).

19. *Ibid.,* p. 162.

20. *Loc. cit.*

21. Burke, *op. cit.,* p. 163.

22. Alexander Gerard, *An Essay on Taste* (1780), facsimile 3rd ed. (Gainesville, Fla.: Scholars' Facsimile and Reprints, 1963), p. 43.

23. Hipple, *op. cit.,* p. 254.

24. Dugald Stewart, *Philosophical Essays* (Edinburgh: 1818), p. 262.

25. Archibald Alison, *Essays on the Nature and Principles of Taste,* selections reprinted in Alexander Sesonske, ed., *What is Art?* (New York: Oxford U. P., 1965), pp. 182–195.

26. *Ibid.,* p. 182.

27. *Ibid.,* p. 193.

28. *Ibid.,* p. 185.

29. David Hume, "Of the Standard of Taste," in *Essays, Literary, Moral, and Political* (London: 1870), pp. 134–149.

30. *Ibid.,* p. 136.

31. *Ibid.,* p. 137.

32. *Ibid.,* p. 138.

33. *Ibid.,* p. 139.

34. *Ibid.,* p. 146.

35. Immanuel Kant, *Critique of Pure Reason,* trans. N. K. Smith (New York: St. Martin's, 1965).

36. Kant's most complete statement of his philosophy of taste is set forth in his *Critique of Judgment,* trans. J. H. Bernard, 2nd ed. (London: 1914). This work is the basis of my account of Kant's aesthetics.

37. Arthur Schopenhauer, *The World as Will and Idea* (London: Routledge and Kegan Paul, 1883), pp. 270–1.

38. Plato, *The Republic of Plato,* trans. F. M. Cornford (New York: Oxford U. P., 1945), pp. 325ff.

39. Plato, *Ion,* trans. W. R. M. Lamb (London: Loeb Library, 1925).

40. Plato, *Phaedrus,* trans. R. Hackforth (Cambridge: Cambridge U. P., 1952), p. 172.

41. Aristotle, *On Poetry and Style,* trans. G. M. A. Grube (Indianapolis: Bobbs-Merrill).

42. *Ibid.,* p. 12.

43. See Grube's discussion of catharsis, *ibid.,* pp. xiv–xvii.

44. Friedrich Nietzsche, *The Will to Power,* vol. II, trans. O. Levy (London: 1910), p. 256.

45. Eugène Véron, *Aesthetics,* trans. W. H. Armstrong (London: 1879), p. 89.

46. Alexander Smith, "The Philosophy of Poetry," reprinted in Sesonske, *op. cit.,* p. 366.

47. Leo Tolstoy, *What is Art?* (Indianapolis: Bobbs-Merrill, 1960), p. 51.

48. See I. A. Richards, *Practical Criticism* (New York: Harcourt Brace, 1929), *The Philosophy of Rhetoric* (New York: Oxford U. P., 1965), *Principles of Literary Criticism* (New York: Harcourt Brace, 1950), pp. 298ff.; Willam Empson, *Seven Types of Ambiguity* (New York: Meridian

Books, 1955); Cleanth Brooks, *The Well Wrought Urn* (New York: Harcourt Brace, 1947); and René Welleck and Austin Warren, *The Theory of Literature* (New York: Harcourt Brace, 1949).

49. Jerome Stolnitz, *Aesthetics and Philosophy of Art Criticism* (Boston: Houghton Mifflin, 1960).

50. Monroe Beardsley, *Aesthetics: Problems in the Philosophy of Criticism* (New York: Harcourt Brace, 1958).

51. See Joseph Margolis, "Aesthetic Perception," *The Journal of Aesthetics and Art Criticism* (1960), pp. 209–213, reprinted in Margolis, *The Language of Art and Art Criticism* (Detroit, Wayne State U. P., 1965), pp. 23–33; and George Dickie, "The Myth of the Aesthetic Attitude," *American Philosophical Quarterly* (1964), pp. 56–65, reprinted in John Hospers, ed., *Introductory Readings in Aesthetics* (New York: Free Press, 1969), pp. 28–44, and in the Bobbs-Merrill Reprint Series in Philosophy.

## Part II

1. Edward Bullough, " 'Psychical Distance' as a Factor in Art and an Aesthetic Principle," reprinted in M. Levich, ed., *Aesthetics and the Philosophy of Criticism* (New York: Random House, 1963), pp. 233–254.

2. Jerome Stolnitz, *Aesthetics and Philosophy of Art Criticism* (Boston: Houghton Mifflin, 1960).

3. Eliseo Vivas, "A Definition of Esthetic Experience," *Journal of Philosophy* (1937), pp. 628–634, reprinted in E. Vivas and M. Krieger, eds., *The Problems of Aesthetics* (New York: Rinehart, 1953), pp. 406–411; Vivas, "Contextualism Reconsidered," *The Journal of Aesthetics and Art Criticism* (1959), pp. 222–240.

4. Virgil Aldrich, *Philosophy of Art* (Englewood Cliffs, N.J.: Prentice-Hall, 1963), pp. 19–27.

5. For examples of theories similar to the attitude theories, see J. O. Urmson, "What Makes a Situation Aesthetic?" *Proc. of the Aristotelian Soc.*, sup. vol. (1957), pp. 75–92, reprinted in J. Margolis, ed., *Philosophy Looks at the Arts* (New York: Scribner's, 1962), pp. 13–27; and V. Tomas, "Aesthetic Vision," *The Philosophical Review* (1959), pp. 52–67.

6. Monroe Beardsley, *Aesthetics* (New York: Harcourt Brace, 1958), pp. 15–65.

7. Bullough, in Levich, *op. cit.*, p. 235.

8. Sheila Dawson, " 'Distancing' as an Aesthetic Principle," *Australasian Journal of Philosophy* (1961), pp. 155–174.

9. Susanne Langer, *Feeling and Form* (New York: Scribner's, 1953).

10. Dawson, *op. cit.*, p. 168.

11. Langer, *op. cit.*, p. 318.

12. Stolnitz, *op. cit.*, pp. 34–35.

13. Vivas, "Contextualism Reconsidered," *op. cit.*, p. 237.

14. Aldrich, *op. cit.*, p. 22.

15. *Loc. cit.*

16. Virgil Aldrich, "Back to Aesthetic Experience," *The Journal of Aesthetics and Art Criticism* (1966), pp. 368–9.

17. For a similar argument see Joseph Margolis's review of Beardsley's *Aesthetics* in *The Journal of Aesthetics and Art Criticism* (1959), p. 267.

18. For a more detailed account of the notion of aesthetic object, see my "Art Narrowly and Broadly Speaking," *American Philosophical Quarterly* (1968), pp. 71–77.

## Part III

1. Clive Bell, *Art* (New York: Capricorn Books, 1958).

2. G. E. Moore, *Principia Ethica* (Cambridge: Cambridge U. P., 1903), Chapter I.

3. *Ibid.*, p. xiii.

4. Bell, *op. cit.*, pp. 16–17.

5. *Ibid.*, p. 17.

6. *Ibid.*, pp. 17–18.

7. *Ibid.*, p. 147.

8. *Ibid.*, p. 20.

9. *Ibid.*, p. 27.

10. Susanne Langer, *Philosophy in a New Key* (New York: New American Library, 1948).

11. Langer, *Feeling and Form* (New York: Scribner's, 1953).

12. Langer, *Problems of Art* (New York: Scribner's, 1957).

13. Langer, *Feeling and Form*, p. 40.

14. Langer, *Problems of Art*, pp. 124–139.

15. Langer, *Feeling and Form*, p. 27.

16. *Ibid.*, pp. 94–95.

17. *Ibid.*, p. xi.

18. *Ibid.*, p. 49.

19. Langer, *Problems of Art*, p. 125.

20. *Ibid.*, p. 133.

21. See especially Ernest Nagel's review of *Philosophy in a New Key*, *Journal of Philosophy* (1943), pp. 323–29.

22. Langer, *Problems of Art*, p. 126.

23. Monroe Beardsley, *Aesthetics* (New York: Harcourt Brace, 1958), p. 336.

24. Langer, *Feeling and Form*, p. 72.

25. *Webster's New Collegiate Dictionary*, 2nd ed. (Springfield, Mass.: 1953).

26. Langer, *Problems of Art*, p. 133.

27. R. G. Collingwood, *The Principles of Art* (New York: Oxford U. P., 1958).

28. *Ibid.*, p. 78.

29. *Ibid.*, p. 278.

30. *Ibid.*, p. 72.

31. *Ibid.*, p. 79.

32. *Ibid.*, p. 108.

33. *Ibid.*, p. 109.

34. *Ibid.*, p. 235.

35. *Ibid.*, p. 229.

36. *Ibid.*, p. 235.

37. *Ibid.*, p. 273.

38. *Ibid.*, pp. 109–110.

39. *Ibid.*, p. 116.

40. *Ibid.*, p. 103.

41. *Ibid.*, p. 118.

42. *Ibid.*, p. 273.

43. Alan Donagan, *The Later Philosophy of R. G. Collingwood* (Oxford: Clarendon, 1962), pp. 116ff.

44. Collingwood, *op. cit.*, p. 280.

45. *Webster's New Collegiate Dictionary.*

46. Collingwood, *op. cit.*, p. 282.

47. *Ibid.*, p. 264.

48. *Ibid.*, p. 336.

49. Morris Weitz, "The Role of Theory in Aesthetics," reprinted in Francis Coleman, ed., *Contemporary Studies in Aesthetics* (New York: McGraw-Hill, 1968), pp. 84–94.

50. *Ibid.*, p. 90.

51. *Loc. cit.*

52. Maurice Mandelbaum, "Family Resemblances and Generalization Concerning the Arts," *American Philosophical Quarterly* (1965), p. 221.

53. *Ibid.*, p. 222.

54. For an earlier discussion of this argument, see my "Defining Art," *American Philosophical Quarterly* (1969), pp. 253–256. This earlier statement is quite brief and needs expansion. The account of the theory presented in this book is somewhat better but it too needs to be expanded and supplemented. I hope soon to publish a longer and more adequate statement of the institutional theory of art.

55. Arthur Danto, "The Artworld," *Journal of Philosophy* (1964), pp. 571–584.

56. *Ibid.*, p. 580.

## Part IV

1. For specific examples of intentionalist criticism see W. K. Wimsatt and Monroe Beardsley, "The Intentional Fallacy," *Sewanee Review* (1946), pp. 468–488 and widely reprinted; and Monroe Beardsley, *Aesthetics* (New York: Harcourt Brace, 1958), pp. 17–29. See also Beardsley, "Textual Meaning and Authorial Meaning," *Genre* (1968), pp. 169–181. For an earlier version of the account presented in this section see my "Meaning and Intention," *Genre* (1968), pp. 182–189. For a defense of intentionalist criticism see E. D. Hirsch, Jr., *Validity in Interpretation* (New Haven: Yale U. P., 1967).

2. Beardsley, *Aesthetics*, p. 458.

3. My account of symbolism in art draws upon Beardsley, *Aesthetics*, pp. 288–293; upon Isabel Hungerland, "Symbols in Poetry," reprinted in W. E. Kennick, ed., *Art and Philosophy* (New York: St. Martin's, 1964), pp. 425–448; and upon Gören Hermerén, *Representation and Meaning in the Visual Arts* (Lund: Berlingska, Boktryckeriet, 1969).

4. Hermerén, *op. cit.*, p. 98.

5. Hungerland, *op. cit.*, p. 427.

6. *Ibid.*, p. 429.

7. *Ibid.*, p. 426.

8. Beardsley, *Aesthetics*, p. 408.

9. My account of metaphor draws on Monroe Beardsley, "The Metaphorical Twist," *Philosophy and Phenomenological Research* (1962), pp. 293–307; and Max Black, "Metaphor," *Proc. of the Aristotelian Soc.* (1954–55), pp. 273–294. Black's article has been reprinted in J. Margolis, ed., *Philosophy Looks at the Arts* (New York: Scribner's, 1962), pp. 218–235.

10. The first three on the list are used as examples by Black, in Margolis, *op. cit.*, p. 219.

11. The fourth example of metaphor is used by Beardsley, in "The Metaphorical Twist," p. 294.

12. For a discussion of these theories see Beardsley, *Aesthetics*, pp. 134–136.

13. Black, in Margolis, *op. cit.*, p. 226.

14. Beardsley, "The Metaphorical Twist," p. 293.

15. *Ibid.*, p. 294.

16. *Ibid.*, pp. 298ff. I have altered Beardsley's argument somewhat by making the significance of the referential aspect of language more explicit and by relating literalness to dictonary senses.

17. Black, in Margolis, *op. cit.*, pp. 229ff.

18. The analysis of expression given here leans heavily on the following: Vincent Tomas, "The Concept of Expression in Art," reprinted in Margolis, *op. cit.*, pp. 30–45; John Hospers, "The Concept of Aesthetic Expression," *Proc. of the Aristotelian Soc.* (1954–55), pp. 313–344; and Monroe Beardsley, *Aesthetics*, pp. 325–332.

## Part V

1. The view set forth here as Beardsley's view is actually a composite of the position developed in his book, *Aesthetics* (New York: Harcourt Brace, 1958) pp. 454–489, and the position developed in his later article, "On the Generality of Critical Reasons," *Journal of Philosophy* (1962), pp. 477–486, also in the Bobbs-Merrill Reprint Series in Philosophy. Where the two positions differ, the later article's line is followed.

2. In private correspondence Beardsley has expressed misgivings about a strict deductive interpretation of his view. In this correspondence he is inclined to think that the relationship between reasons and evaluations is somewhat looser than a deductive one. The reader is thus warned that Beardsley does not endorse all aspects of the view that I am here calling "Beardsley's theory." The deductive interpretation of Beardsley's theory is based on his article, "On the Generality of Critical Reasons"; the earlier account of evaluation he gave in his book was not deductive in nature.

3. Beardsley, "On the Generality of Critical Reasons," p. 485.

4. *Loc. cit.*

5. *Loc. cit.*

6. Obviously the critic's remarks at this point could and ought to be greatly expanded. For a detailed discussion of this and many other of Cézanne's paintings, see Erle Loran, *Cézanne's Composition* (Berkeley: U. of Calif. P., 1963).

7. Beardsley, "On the Generality of Critical Reasons," p. 477.

8. Beardsley, *Aesthetics,* p. 528.

9. *Loc. cit.*

10. Beardsley, *Aesthetics,* p. 529.

11. See my "Beardsley's Phantom Aesthetic Experience," *Journal of Philosophy* (1965), pp.129–136, for a criticism of Beardsley's notion of a unity of experience. See Beardsley's reply, "Aesthetic Experience Regained," *The Journal of Aesthetics and Art Criticism* (1969), pp. 3–11.

12. Beardsley, *Aesthetics,* p. 530.

13. *Ibid.,* p. 531.

14. For examples, see C. J. Ducasse, *The Philosophy of Art* (New York: Dial, 1929), Chapters 14 and 15; and George Boas, *A Primer for Critics* (Baltimore: Johns Hopkins U. P., 1937), Chapters 1 and 3.

15. G. E. Moore, *Principia Ethica* (Cambridge: Cambridge U. P., 1903), Chapter 1.

16. For examples of Platonistic theories see C. E. M. Joad, *Matter, Life and Value* (London: Oxford U. P., 1929), pp. 266–283, in part reprinted in E. Vivas and M. Krieger, eds., *Problems of Aesthetics* (New York: Rinehart, 1953), pp. 463–479; Harold Osborne, *Theory of Beauty* (London: Routledge and Kegan Paul, 1952); and T. E. Jessop, "The Definition of Beauty," *Proc. of the Aristotelian Soc.* (1933), pp. 159–172.

17. A. J. Ayer, *Language, Truth, and Logic* (New York: Dover, 1946), pp. 102–114.

18. C. L. Stevenson, *Ethics and Language* (New Haven: Yale U. P., 1944).

19. R. M. Hare, *The Language of Morals* (New York: Oxford U. P., 1964), and *Freedom and Reason* (Oxford: Clarendon, 1963).

20. Bernard Heyl, *New Bearings in Esthetics and Art Criticism* (New Haven: Yale U. P., 1943).

21. For examples see Arnold Isenberg, "Critical Communication," reprinted in W. Elton ed., *Aesthetics and Language* (New York: Philosophical Library, 1954), pp. 131–146; and Stuart Hampshire, "Logic and Appreciation," reprinted in Elton, pp. 161–169.

22. Mary Mothersill, " 'Unique' as an Aesthetic Predicate," *Journal of Philosophy* (1961), pp. 421–437; reprinted in F. Coleman, ed., *Contemporary Studies in Aesthetics* (New York: McGraw-Hill, 1968), pp. 193–208.

23. Mothersill, "Critical Reasons," *The Philosophical Quarterly* (1961), pp. 74–78; reprinted in Coleman, *op. cit.,* pp. 209–213.

# Bibliography

## Primary Sources

Aldrich, Virgil, *Philosophy of Art.* Englewood Cliffs, N. J.: Prentice-Hall, 1963.

Beardsley, Monroe, *Aesthetics.* New York: Harcourt Brace, 1958. See the magnificent annotated bibliography in this book.

————. *Aesthetics from Classical Greece to the Present.* New York: Macmillan, 1966.

Bell, Clive. *Art.* New York: Capricorn Books, 1958.

Collingwood, R. G. *The Principles of Art.* New York: Oxford U. P., 1958.

Croce, Benedetto. *Aesthetic.* Trans. Douglas Ainslie, 2nd ed. New York: Macmillan, 1922.

Dewey, John. *Art as Experience.* New York: Minton, Balch, 1934.

Greene, T. M. *The Arts and the Art of Criticism.* Princeton: Princeton U. P., 1947.

Hermerén, Gören. *Representation and Meaning in the Visual Arts.* Lund: Berlingska, Boktryckeriet, 1969.

Heyl, Bernard. *New Bearings in Esthetics and Art Criticism.* New Haven: Yale U. P., 1943.

Hipple, Jr., Walter J. *The Beautiful, the Sublime, and the Picturesque in Eighteenth-Century British Aesthetic Theory.* Carbondale, Ill.: Southern Illinois U. P., 1957.

Hospers, John. *Meaning and Truth in the Arts.* Chapel Hill, N.C.: University of North Carolina Press, 1946.

Langer, Suzanne. *Feeling and Form.* New York: Scribner's, 1953.

————. *Philosophy in a New Key.* New York: New American Library, 1948.

————. *Problems of Art.* New York: Scribner's, 1957.

Langfeld, Herbert S. *The Aesthetic Attitude.* New York: Harcourt Brace, 1920.

Margolis, Joseph. *The Language of Art and Art Criticism.* Detroit: Wayne State U. P., 1965.

————. "Recent Work in Aesthetics," *American Philosophical Quarterly,* 1965, pp. 182–192.

Mead, Hunter. *An Introduction to Aesthetics.* New York: Ronald, 1952.

Moore, G. E. *Principia Ethica*. Cambridge: Cambridge U. P., 1903.

Osborne, Harold. *Aesthetics and Criticism*. London: Routledge and Kegan Paul, 1955.

————. *Theory of Beauty*. London: Routledge and Kegan Paul, 1952.

Parker, DeWitt. *The Principles of Aesthetics*, 2nd ed. New York: Appleton-Century-Crofts, 1920.

————. *The Analysis of Art*. New Haven: Yale U. P., 1926.

Pepper, Stephen. *The Basis of Criticism in the Arts*. Cambridge, Mass.: Harvard U. P., 1949.

————. *The Work of Art*. Bloomington, Ind.: Indiana U. P., 1955.

Prall, David W. *Aesthetic Analysis*. New York: Crowell, 1936.

————. *Aesthetic Judgment*. New York: Crowell, 1929.

Santayana, George. *The Sense of Beauty*. New York: Modern Library, 1955.

Stolnitz, Jerome. *Aesthetics and Philosophy of Art Criticism*. Boston: Houghton Mifflin, 1960.

Vivas, Eliseo. *The Artistic Transaction*. Columbus, Ohio: Ohio State U. P., 1963.

————. *Creation and Discovery*. New York: Noonday, 1955.

Weitz, Morris. *Philosophy of the Arts*. Cambridge, Mass.: Harvard U. P., 1950.

Wittgenstein, Ludwig. *Philosophical Investigations*. Trans. G. E. M. Anscombe. New York: Macmillan, 1953.

## Anthologies

Aschenbrenner, K. and A. Isenberg, eds. *Aesthetic Theories: Studies in the Philosophy of Art*. Englewood Cliffs, N.J.: Prentice-Hall, 1965.

Coleman, Francis, ed. *Contemporary Studies in Aesthetics*. New York: McGraw-Hill, 1968.

Beardsley, M. and H. Schueller, eds. *Aesthetic Inquiry: Essays on Art Criticism and the Philosophy of Art*. Belmont, Calif.: Dickerson, 1967.

Elton, William, ed. *Aesthetics and Language*. New York: Philosophical Library, 1954.

Hofstadter, A. and Richard Kuhns, eds. *Philosophies of Art and Beauty*. New York: Modern Library, 1964.

Hospers, John, ed. *Introductory Readings in Aesthetics*. New York: Free Press, 1969.

Kennick, W. E., ed. *Art and Philosophy*. New York: St. Martin's, 1964.

Levich, Marvin, ed. *Aesthetics and the Philosophy of Criticism*. New York: Random House, 1963.

Margolis, Joseph, ed. *Philosophy Looks at the Arts*. New York: Scribner's, 1962.

Philipson, Morris, ed. *Aesthetics Today*. New York: Meridian Books, 1961.

Rader, Melvin, ed. *A Modern Book of Esthetics*, 3rd ed. Holt, 1960.

Richter, Peyton, ed. *Perspectives in Aesthetics*. New York: Odyssey, 1967.

Sesonske, Alexander, ed. *What is Art? Aesthetic Theory from Plato to Tolstoy*. New York: Oxford U. P., 1965.

Tillman, F. and S. Cahn, eds. *Philosophy of Art and Aesthetics*. New York: Harper and Row, 1969.

Vivas, Eliseo and Murry Krieger, eds. *The Problems of Aesthetics*. New York: Rinehart, 1953.

Weitz, Morris, ed. *Problems in Aesthetics*. New York: Macmillan, 1959.

# Index

abstraction, 78, 79, 80
accidental art, 110
Addison, J., 23
aesthetically pleasing, 59
aesthetically relevant, 60
aesthetic appreciation, 28, 49, 105;
    attitude theory, 12, 18, 44, 45, 46,
    47–60, 61, 66, 67, 68; concept of,
    30, 53, 47–68; emotion, 72, 73, 76,
    77; experience, 45, 58, 60, 68, 153–
    57, 182; goodness, 147, 156; ob-
    ject, 45, 47–68, 95, 142, 153, 155,
    156, 161; perception, 56–59;
    space, 58; the —, 32, 47–68, 109;
    theory, 11–12, 31, 43–45, 68, 70
"aesthetics," the term, 26; defined,
    52; origin of, 9–10
aesthetic value, 58, 153, 159, 160,
    165 (see evaluation); defined, 156;
    instrumental theory of, 148, 152,
    153–59, 160, 175, 180, 182; pri-
    mary criteria of, 150, 153, 154
    (see complexity, intensity, and
    unity); secondary criteria of, 150,
    153
agreeable, the, 30
agreeable emotion, 22
Alberti, L. B., 9, 183
Aldrich, V., x, 48, 56–59, 185
Alison, A., 2, 19, 20–23, 30, 184
ambiguous figures, 56, 57, 58
ambiguous sentences, 113–19; and
    discourse condition, 116; and
    language community, 115, 116,
    117; and linguistic environment,

ambiguous sentences—*cont.*
    114; and nonlinguistic condi-
    tions, 113, 114, 117, 118, 119
amusement art, 86, 87
Anatidae, 114, 117
Apollonian qualities, 40
appreciation, 104, 105; aesthetic,
    28, 49, 105; candidate for, 101–
    05, 108; defined, 101
Aquinas, T., 7–8, 183
Aristotle, 2, 7, 32, 33, 82, 87, 107,
    132, 184; conception of art, 36;
    poetic theory of, 35–38
art, accidental, 110; amusement,
    86, 87; artifactuality and, 97, 98,
    100, 101, 106, 107; Aristotle's
    conception of, 36; as illusion, 34;
    as imaginative expression, 84; as
    open concept, 70, 95–98; as a
    social institution, 98–108; bad,
    84, 91, 92, 104–05, 121, 159; Bell's
    theory of, 70–78; classificatory
    sense of, 43, 62, 76, 94, 98, 99,
    100, 101, 106; Collingwood's
    theory of, 84–95, 140; emotional
    nature of, 34–35; evaluation of
    (see theories of evaluation); eval-
    uative sense of, 43, 76, 94, 98, 99,
    100; expression theory of, 33, 37,
    38–41, 42, 69, 70, 78, 140; found,
    105; generic concept of, 96, 97,
    98; good, 84, 91, 92, 121; imita-
    tion theory of, 32, 38, 41, 42, 69,
    81; institutional theory of, 70, 98–
    108; intention and the evalua-